NMLS STUDY GUIDE

The Most Complete Mortgage Loan Originator Test Prep with 8 Full-Length MLO Practice Exams and 1000+ Questions with Detailed Answer Explanations. Boost Your Career!

Jeremy Crainstone

© 2024 The Most Comprehensive NMLS Study Guide All rights reserved. This guide is for informational use only. Trademarks and brand names are owned by their respective holders. Provided "as is," without warranties. The publisher is not liable for any damages from use or misuse of the content. Unauthorized reproduction, distribution, or transmission of this book is strictly prohibited.

Table of Contents

Introduction 10
   NMLS Exam Overview 10
   Importance of the NMLS Exam 11
   NMLS Licensing Process Overview 12
Chapter 1: Federal Mortgage Laws 15
   Real Estate Settlement Procedures Act 15
      RESPA Origins and Purpose 15
      Mortgage Broker Definition and Role 16
      Applicable Loan Types 17
      RESPA Prohibitions & Exemptions 18
      Settlement Services and RESPA Compliance 19
      Required Borrower Information (Reg X) 20
      Foreclosure Process and RESPA Obligations 21
      Initial Escrow Statements Explained 23
   Equal Credit Opportunity Act (ECOA) 24
      ECOA Permissible Lender Actions 24
      Prohibited Discrimination Factors 26
      Loan Denial: Valid Reasons 27
      Regulation B: Lender Obligations Under ECOA 28
      Notifying Borrowers of Credit Decisions 30
      Required Disclosures for Denied Applications 31
      Adverse Action: Definition and Notifications 32
      Application Data & ECOA's Elderly Definition 33
      MLO Reporting When Borrower Declines Info 34
      Co-signer Requirements Explained 36
      Acceptable Income for Loan Review 37
      Creditworthiness Factors 38
   Truth in Lending Act (TILA) 39

- Purpose of TILA 39
- Loans Covered Under TILA 41
- Key Terms: APR, Finance Charge, Dwelling, Loan 42
- Right to Rescind and Seller Contributions 43
- HOEPA Protections for High-Cost Mortgages 44
- Higher-Priced Mortgage Loan Criteria 45
- MLO Compensation Rules and Restrictions 47

TILA-RESPA Integrated Disclosure Rule 48
- Purpose of TRID 48
- Loans Covered Under TRID 49
- Loan Estimate Breakdown 50
- Loan Consummation Definition 52
- CFPB Toolkit Delivery Requirements 53
- Closing Disclosure Contents 53
- Disclosures Timing Rules 55
- MLO Actions for Incomplete TRID Disclosure 56
- Change of Circumstances in Loan Estimates 57
- Consumer Rights: Loan Information Requests 58
- Borrower's Right to Rescission 60
- Annual Escrow Statement Overview 61

Other Federal Laws and Guidelines 61
- Home Mortgage Disclosure Act (HMDA) Overview 61
- Fair Credit Reporting and Consumer Rights 63
- Federal Trade Commission Red Flag Rules 64
- BSA/AML: MLO Reporting and Compliance 65
- Gramm-Leach-Bliley Act: Privacy & Compliance 67
- Mortgage Advertising Regulations 68
- E-Sign Act: Rules and Legal Equivalence 69
- USA PATRIOT Act: Identity Verification & Reporting 70

- Homeowners' Protection Act: PMI Cancellation 72
- Dodd-Frank Act: CFPB and Lending Standards 73
- Regulatory Authority 74
  - CFPB's Role in Mortgage Law Enforcement 74
  - HUD: Fair Housing and FHA Loan Regulation 75

Chapter 2: Uniform State Content 78
- SAFE Act 78
  - SAFE Act: Purpose and Scope 78
  - Public Record Filing Requirements 79
- State Mortgage Regulatory Agencies 80
  - Regulatory Powers and Responsibilities 80
  - NMLS Registry and State Regulators 82
  - Frequency of Exams 83
  - MLO Unique Identifiers and Their Purpose 84
  - CFPB Loan Originator Rule: Dual Compensation 85
- License Law and Regulation 87
  - Licensing Requirements for MLOs 87
  - MLO-Licensed Services Overview 88
  - Allowable Activities Without MLO License 89
  - Entities Requiring Licensed MLOs 91
  - Exemptions for Depository Institutions 92
  - Licensee Qualifications & Application Process 93
  - Test Retake Waiting Periods 95
  - Sponsorship Requirement for MLOs 95
  - Definition of MLO 97
  - Grounds for Denying a License 98
  - License Maintenance Essentials 99
  - NMLS Employment & Identifier Requirements 100
  - Temporary Authority for MLOs 101

Compliance 103
    Regulator's Authority to Audit and Interview 103
    Prohibited Acts in Real Estate Transactions 104
    Required Conduct in Complaint Investigations 105
    Assumable Loan Scenarios and Conditions 106
    Permissible MLO Activities 107
    Penalties for Noncompliance 108
    General Loan Origination Scenarios 109
    NMLS Identifier in Advertising 111

Chapter 3: General Mortgage Knowledge 113
Qualified vs. Non-qualified Mortgage Programs 113
    Qualified Mortgages and ATR Compliance 113
    Conforming Loans: Fannie Mae and Freddie Mac 114
    Government-Backed Loans: FHA, VA, USDA 115
    Nonconforming and Nontraditional Mortgages 116

Mortgage Loan Products 118
    Fixed-Rate Mortgages Explained 118
    Adjustable-Rate Mortgages Explained 119
    Purchase Money Second Mortgages 120
    Balloon Mortgages: Risks and Refinancing 121
    Reverse Mortgages: Eligibility and Risks 122
    Home Equity Line of Credit (HELOC) 123
    Construction Mortgages Explained 124
    Interest-Only Mortgages Explained 126

Mortgage Industry Terminology 127
    Loan Terms and Concepts Explained 127
    Disclosure Terms in Mortgage Lending 128
    Financial Terms Explained 129
    General Terms: Subordination to APR 131

Chapter 4: Mortgage Loan Origination 133
Loan Inquiry and Application Process 133
Loan Inquiry Disclosures 133
Borrower Application Process 134
Verification Steps for Loan Applications 135
Suitability of Loan Products & Programs 136
Accuracy and Tolerance in Service Charges 137
Disclosure Timing Rules 138
Loan Estimate Timing and Corrections 140
Closing Disclosure & Counseling Info 141
Qualification: Processing & Underwriting 142
Borrower Analysis: Evaluating Financial Health 142
Appraisals: Purpose, Approaches, Timing 144
Title Reports and Commitments 145
Insurance: Flood, PMI, Hazard, Government 146
Closing 148
Title Insurance and Its Importance 148
Settlement Agent & Valid Signatures 149
Explanation of Closing Cost Components 150
Required Closing Documents 151
Funding Procedures and Rescission Periods 152
Financial Calculations 154
Calculating Periodic Interest 154
Monthly Payment Calculations 155
Calculating Required Down Payments 156
Estimating Closing Costs and Prepaids 157
ARM Adjustments: Rates and Payments 159
Chapter 5: Ethics 161
Ethical Issues 161

    Prohibited Acts and MLO Duties 161

    Fair Lending Practices and Compliance 162

    Fraud Detection and Red Flags 163

    Identifying Suspicious Bank Activities 164

    Advertising Compliance and UDAAP Standards 165

    Predatory Lending and Steering Practices 167

Ethical Behavior in Loan Origination 168

    Financial Responsibility and Fee Regulations 168

    Handling Borrower Complaints 169

    Mortgage Company Compliance Obligations 171

Relationships with Consumers 172

    Protecting Consumer Data and Cybersecurity 172

    Disclosing Changes and Validating Eligibility 173

    Income Verification and Ethical Practices 174

    Truthful Marketing and Advertising Compliance 175

    General Business Ethics 177

Conclusion 179

    Acknowledgments 179

    Encouragement and Motivation in Mortgages 179

READ THIS PAGE CAREFULLY BEFORE YOU START PREPARING FOR THE EXAM

By purchasing this book, you gain access to a wealth of additional resources designed to help you prepare effectively. Don't think of your purchase as limited to the physical book in your hands—take advantage of all the extra resources available to you.

After consulting with many students who failed their exams, we identified a common issue: THESE STUDENTS WERE NOT ACCUSTOMED TO TAKING THE EXAM ONLINE. This is a critical problem, as the exam is computer-based, meaning you must train under similar conditions to the actual exam. Otherwise, your chances of passing are significantly reduced.

FOR THIS REASON, WE CHOSE NOT TO INCLUDE PRACTICE EXERCISES IN THE BOOK but instead provide them in digital format. This approach will help you familiarize yourself with the digital exam format. While this may feel challenging at first, it greatly increases your chances of success.

Happy studying!

SCAN THE QR CODE:

Introduction

NMLS Exam Overview

The **NMLS Exam**, formally known as the **SAFE Mortgage Loan Originator Test**, plays a pivotal role in the professional journey of aspiring mortgage loan originators (MLOs). It serves as a critical gateway for individuals seeking to enter the mortgage industry, ensuring that only those with a comprehensive understanding of federal and state laws, mortgage procedures, and ethical practices are granted the license to operate. This exam is mandated by the Secure and Fair Enforcement for Mortgage Licensing Act of 2008 (SAFE Act), which aims to enhance consumer protection and reduce fraud by setting minimum standards for the licensing and registration of state-licensed mortgage loan originators.

The NMLS Exam is divided into two main components: the **National Component** and the **State Component**. The National Component covers a wide range of topics essential for every MLO, including federal mortgage-related laws such as the Truth in Lending Act (TILA), the Real Estate Settlement Procedures Act (RESPA), and regulations on mortgage origination activities, ethics, and the overall mortgage process. It tests candidates on their knowledge of mortgage industry practices, ethical considerations, and federal compliance requirements. The State Component, on the other hand, focuses on specific regulations and laws applicable to mortgage origination in individual states, ensuring that MLOs are well-versed in the nuances of their local mortgage market.

The content requirements for the NMLS Exam are extensive and designed to assess the candidate's mastery of key concepts critical to the practice of mortgage loan origination. These include understanding loan products and terms, the ability to calculate mortgage payments and costs, knowledge of federal laws and regulations governing the mortgage industry, and the application of ethical practices in mortgage loan origination. Additionally, the exam tests the candidate's understanding of the mortgage market, including the roles of various entities involved in the mortgage lending process, such as lenders, underwriters, and settlement agents.

Preparation for the NMLS Exam requires a thorough study of the aforementioned topics, along with a deep dive into the specifics of mortgage processes, from application to closing. Candidates must also familiarize themselves with the legal and regulatory environment of the mortgage industry, including recent changes and updates to laws and regulations. This comprehensive preparation ensures that licensed mortgage loan originators are not only proficient in the technical aspects of mortgage lending but also committed to upholding the highest ethical standards in their professional conduct.

Success in the NMLS Exam signifies a significant milestone in the career of a mortgage professional. It not only demonstrates the individual's dedication and expertise in the field of mortgage lending but also instills confidence in consumers, knowing that they are dealing with a licensed professional who is knowledgeable and adheres to a strict code of ethics. For those aspiring to excel in the mortgage industry, passing the NMLS Exam is a crucial step towards achieving career advancement, personal fulfillment, and the opportunity to contribute to the integrity and professionalism of the mortgage lending process.

Importance of the NMLS Exam

Passing the NMLS exam is a pivotal step for any individual aspiring to become a licensed Mortgage Loan Originator (MLO). This certification is not merely a formality but a crucial benchmark that signifies the individual's comprehensive understanding and adherence to the rigorous standards set forth by the mortgage industry. The importance of this exam extends beyond the legal requirement; it is a testament to the individual's commitment to professionalism, ethical practices, and a deep understanding of the complexities of mortgage lending.

Legal Certification and Compliance: The first and most obvious reason for the importance of the NMLS exam is its role in legal certification. The Secure and Fair Enforcement for Mortgage Licensing Act of 2008 (SAFE Act) mandates this exam for all mortgage loan originators seeking state licensure. This legal framework ensures that only qualified individuals who have demonstrated a thorough understanding of federal and state mortgage laws, as well as ethical and operational standards, can advise consumers on mortgage loans. Compliance with these regulations is not optional but a strict requirement. Passing the NMLS exam is the gateway to becoming a part of the mortgage industry, ensuring that all licensed MLOs meet the minimum standards for consumer protection and fraud prevention.

Career Advancement: Beyond the legal requirements, the NMLS exam is a cornerstone for career advancement within the mortgage industry. Achieving a passing score on this exam is often seen as a significant professional milestone. It opens doors to numerous opportunities, from working with reputable mortgage companies to advancing to higher positions within the industry. The knowledge and skills verified by this exam are invaluable assets that enhance an MLO's credibility and marketability. In a competitive field, being a licensed MLO can set an individual apart, showcasing their dedication to their profession and their capability to perform at the highest standards.

Ensuring Industry Compliance: The mortgage industry is characterized by its dynamic regulatory environment. Mortgage loan originators must stay abreast of the latest laws, regulations, and guidelines that govern their practice. The NMLS exam covers a broad spectrum of these regulatory topics, ensuring that MLOs have a solid foundation in the legal aspects of mortgage lending. This knowledge is critical not only for passing the exam but for navigating the complexities of mortgage transactions on a daily basis. Compliance is a key concern for mortgage companies, and having a team of well-informed, licensed MLOs is essential to maintaining the integrity and legality of their operations.

Consumer Protection and Trust: At the heart of the NMLS exam's importance is the protection of consumers. The mortgage process can be complex and daunting for many individuals. Licensed MLOs, having passed the NMLS exam, are equipped to guide consumers through this process with expertise and ethical consideration. This not only serves to protect consumers from potential fraud and exploitation but also builds trust between MLOs and their clients. The assurance that comes from dealing with a licensed professional cannot be overstated; it fosters a positive, transparent, and secure mortgage lending experience.

Professional Growth and Personal Fulfillment: Lastly, passing the NMLS exam contributes to an individual's professional growth and personal fulfillment. The preparation for this exam involves rigorous study and a deep dive into the nuances of mortgage lending. Achieving a passing score is a significant accomplishment that reflects an individual's hard work, dedication, and mastery of the subject matter. This achievement can be a source of personal pride and a stepping stone to further professional development and specialization within the industry.

In conclusion, the NMLS exam is much more than a regulatory hurdle. It is a critical component of a mortgage loan originator's professional journey, underscoring the importance of legal certification, career advancement, industry compliance, consumer protection, and personal achievement. For those aspiring to excel in the mortgage industry, passing this exam is an indispensable step toward realizing their goals and contributing to the professionalism and integrity of the field.

NMLS Licensing Process Overview

The NMLS licensing process is a structured pathway designed to ensure that Mortgage Loan Originators (MLOs) meet the necessary qualifications and adhere to the standards set forth by the Secure and Fair Enforcement for Mortgage Licensing Act of 2008 (SAFE Act). The process encompasses several key steps, each of which must be completed successfully to obtain licensure. These steps include the completion of pre-license education, passing the NMLS exam, submitting an application through the Nationwide Multistate Licensing System & Registry (NMLS), undergoing a background check, and satisfying any state-specific requirements.

Pre-License Education: The first step in the NMLS licensing process involves completing pre-license education courses. These courses are designed to provide candidates with a comprehensive understanding of federal and state mortgage laws, loan origination activities, ethics, and the overall mortgage process. The SAFE Act mandates a minimum of 20 hours of pre-license education, which includes 3 hours of federal law and regulations, 3 hours of ethics, 2 hours of training on standards related to nontraditional mortgage products, and 12 hours of elective education on mortgage origination.

NMLS Exam: After completing the required pre-license education, candidates must pass the NMLS exam, which is divided into two components: the National Component and the State Component. The National Component tests the candidate's knowledge of federal laws, general mortgage knowledge, mortgage loan origination activities, and ethics. The State Component focuses on state-specific laws and regulations. Candidates must achieve a passing score on both components to move forward in the licensing process.

Application Submission: Once the NMLS exam has been successfully passed, candidates must submit an application for licensure through the NMLS. This application requires detailed personal and professional information, including employment history, residential history, and any disciplinary actions within the financial services industry.

Background Check and Fingerprinting: As part of the application process, candidates are required to undergo a background check and submit fingerprints. The background check is conducted to ensure that candidates have not been involved in any criminal activities that would disqualify them from obtaining licensure. The fingerprinting process aids in the verification of the candidate's identity and the completion of the background check.

Credit Report: Applicants must authorize the NMLS to obtain a credit report as part of the licensing process. The credit report is reviewed to assess the financial responsibility of the candidate, as financial irresponsibility could be deemed a risk to consumers.

State-Specific Requirements: In addition to the steps mentioned above, some states may have additional requirements for licensure. These can include state-specific pre-license education, passing a state-specific law exam, or completing a certain number of hours of continuing education each year to maintain licensure. Candidates are advised to review the requirements of the state in which they wish to obtain licensure to ensure compliance with all state-specific regulations.

Sponsorship: Before an MLO license is activated, candidates must be sponsored by an employer who is also registered or licensed through the NMLS. This sponsorship indicates that the candidate is employed by a company that is compliant with state and federal regulations governing mortgage lending.

Upon successful completion of all these steps, candidates are granted an MLO license, which is a critical milestone in their professional journey as mortgage loan originators. This license must be maintained through the completion of annual continuing education requirements and compliance with state and federal mortgage laws and regulations. The NMLS licensing process is designed to ensure that MLOs possess the necessary knowledge, skills, and ethical standards to effectively serve consumers in the mortgage industry.

Chapter 1: Federal Mortgage Laws

Real Estate Settlement Procedures Act

RESPA Origins and Purpose

The Real Estate Settlement Procedures Act (RESPA), enacted in 1974, emerged as a pivotal piece of legislation aimed at revolutionizing the real estate settlement process in the United States. Its creation was motivated by a pressing need to address and mitigate unethical practices that were rampant in the real estate industry, particularly those related to the lack of disclosure regarding settlement costs and the prevalence of kickbacks and referral fees that served to inflate the costs of real estate transactions for consumers. These practices not only compromised the integrity of the real estate market but also placed an undue financial burden on consumers, who were often left in the dark about the true costs and the mechanics of their mortgage transactions.

At its core, RESPA was designed to foster greater transparency in the real estate settlement process. This was achieved by mandating the provision of detailed disclosures to consumers at various stages of the loan application and settlement process, thereby empowering them with the information necessary to make informed decisions. One of the hallmark features of RESPA is the requirement for lenders to provide a Good Faith Estimate (GFE) of settlement costs to applicants within three days of receiving a loan application. This estimate serves to inform consumers of the expected costs associated with their mortgage, including but not limited to, lender fees, title charges, and escrow payments. Additionally, RESPA obligates lenders to furnish borrowers with a HUD-1 Settlement Statement at least one day before the closing of the loan. This statement itemizes the actual charges that will be paid by or on behalf of the borrower, offering a transparent comparison between the initially quoted estimates and the final settlement charges.

Another significant aspect of RESPA's purpose is its stringent prohibition against kickbacks, referral fees, and unearned fees. These provisions were specifically designed to eliminate practices that could lead to unnecessary increases in the costs of settlement services. Under RESPA, no person can give or accept any fee, kickback, or thing of value in exchange for the referral of settlement service business. This prohibition extends to unearned fees, ensuring that all charges for settlement services are justified by services that are actually rendered.

Furthermore, RESPA enhances consumer protection by addressing issues related to the servicing of mortgage loans. It sets forth requirements for the timely and proper handling of borrowers' escrow accounts, mandates servicers to provide timely responses to borrowers' inquiries, and outlines procedures for the management and resolution of complaints regarding the servicing of loans. These provisions underscore RESPA's overarching aim to protect consumers from practices that could jeopardize their financial well-being or lead to unwarranted complications in the management of their mortgage loans.

In summary, the enactment of RESPA marked a significant step forward in the effort to ensure fairness, transparency, and ethical practices within the real estate settlement process. By addressing key issues such as undisclosed costs, kickbacks, and the mishandling of loan servicing, RESPA has played a crucial role in safeguarding the interests of consumers and restoring confidence in the real estate market. Its ongoing relevance and applicability underscore the enduring need for regulatory measures that prioritize consumer protection and promote integrity in real estate transactions.

Mortgage Broker Definition and Role

A mortgage broker acts as an intermediary between borrowers seeking to secure a mortgage and lenders offering those financial products. Their primary role is to assess the borrower's financial situation, which includes evaluating credit history, employment status, assets, and liabilities, to determine the most suitable loan options available from various lenders. By comparing rates, terms, and fees across a range of mortgage offerings, mortgage brokers can tailor recommendations to the specific needs and financial goals of the borrower.

Compensation for mortgage brokers typically comes in the form of a commission or fee for their services. This compensation can be paid by the borrower, the lender, or a combination of both, depending on the agreement and the regulations governing mortgage transactions in the jurisdiction. It's important to note that the Real Estate Settlement Procedures Act (RESPA) plays a significant role in how mortgage brokers are compensated. RESPA prohibits the payment of kickbacks or referral fees that could increase the cost of the mortgage transaction for the consumer. Under RESPA guidelines, any compensation to the mortgage broker must be for services actually performed and must not be tied to the interest rate or terms of the loan they secure for the borrower.

RESPA's guidelines ensure transparency in the mortgage process, requiring that borrowers receive timely and clear disclosures about the nature and cost of the real estate settlement process. Mortgage brokers, therefore, must provide borrowers with a detailed account of their services, the fees associated with these services, and how they will be paid. This clarity helps borrowers make informed decisions and protects them from potentially predatory lending practices.

The role of the mortgage broker under RESPA guidelines is to serve the best interest of the borrower by providing a wide range of loan options, facilitating the application process, and ensuring that all compensation and fees are transparent and justified. This regulatory framework ensures that the mortgage brokerage industry operates with integrity, promoting fair and competitive lending practices that benefit consumers.

Applicable Loan Types

The Real Estate Settlement Procedures Act (RESPA) applies to a wide range of loan types, primarily focusing on those related to residential real estate transactions. Understanding the scope of **federally related mortgage loans** and **government-insured loans** covered under RESPA, as well as recognizing the exemptions such as **business loans** and **temporary financing**, is crucial for mortgage loan originators to ensure compliance and provide accurate guidance to borrowers.

Federally related mortgage loans encompass most loans secured by a lien on residential properties. These are loans intended for one to four-family units, and include purchases, refinances, lender-approved assumptions, property improvement loans, equity lines of credit, and reverse mortgages. Federally related mortgage loans are broad in scope, covering loans made by lenders such as banks, credit unions, and online lenders that are insured, guaranteed, supplemented, or even owned by a federal government agency like the FHA (Federal Housing Administration) or VA (Veterans Affairs).

Government-insured loans are a subset of federally related mortgage loans, specifically those insured by federal agencies to reduce the risk of lender loss in the case of borrower default. FHA loans, VA loans, and USDA (United States Department of Agriculture) loans fall into this category. FHA loans are popular for their lower down payment requirements and are accessible to borrowers with less-than-perfect credit scores. VA loans offer benefits to veterans and active military members, including no down payment or private mortgage insurance (PMI) requirements. USDA loans are targeted at rural property buyers, offering 100% financing for eligible properties and borrowers.

However, RESPA does not apply to all types of financing. **Exemptions** include **business loans**, which are primarily for commercial or agricultural purposes, and not secured by residential real estate. Similarly, **temporary financing**, such as construction loans intended for the short-term financing of building a home, are not covered under RESPA. These exemptions are critical for mortgage professionals to understand, as they delineate the boundaries of RESPA's applicability, ensuring that loan originators can accurately navigate compliance requirements.

A thorough comprehension of the loan types covered under RESPA, alongside an awareness of the exemptions, is indispensable for mortgage loan originators. This knowledge not only aids in maintaining regulatory compliance but also equips professionals to offer precise and reliable advice to clients navigating the complexities of mortgage financing.

RESPA Prohibitions & Exemptions

The Real Estate Settlement Procedures Act (RESPA) establishes specific prohibitions, limitations, and exemptions designed to protect consumers during the mortgage process. A critical aspect of RESPA is its stance against kickbacks and unearned fees. Under RESPA, it is illegal for anyone involved in the settlement process to receive or pay fees that are not for services actually rendered. This prohibition is aimed at eliminating under-the-table payments that could inflate the cost of mortgage settlement services for consumers. For instance, a mortgage broker cannot legally receive a payment for referring a borrower to a particular title company unless that payment is for actual services performed and not merely for the referral.

RESPA also addresses the issue of unearned fees. Fees charged to the borrower must correspond to services that are actually performed. This means that fees for services not rendered or duplicated fees are not permissible under RESPA. The act ensures that all charges to the borrower are for legitimate and necessary services related to the mortgage transaction.

The act mandates several required disclosures to help consumers understand the nature and costs of the real estate settlement process. One of the key disclosures is the Good Faith Estimate (GFE), which provides borrowers with an itemized list of estimated settlement charges they are likely to incur. Another important disclosure is the HUD-1 Settlement Statement, which itemizes the actual charges imposed on borrowers and sellers in connection with the settlement. These disclosures are designed to ensure transparency and to allow consumers to shop for certain settlement services.

RESPA includes specific tolerances for the difference between estimated and actual settlement charges. Certain charges cannot increase at settlement, while others may not increase by more than 10 percent, ensuring that borrowers are not surprised by significantly higher costs than initially quoted.

However, RESPA does provide exemptions for certain types of transactions. Commercial properties and all-cash deals, for instance, are not covered by RESPA. This exemption means that the purchase of commercial real estate and residential transactions conducted without mortgage financing do not require the disclosures and are not subject to the prohibitions and limitations set forth in RESPA. This distinction underscores the act's focus on residential mortgage borrowing, where consumers are deemed to need protection from potential abuses in the settlement process.

Understanding the intricacies of RESPA's prohibitions, limitations, and exemptions is crucial for mortgage loan originators. This knowledge not only ensures compliance with federal law but also equips professionals to advise their clients accurately on the costs and procedures involved in the mortgage settlement process. By adhering to RESPA's guidelines, mortgage professionals help uphold the integrity of the real estate market and protect consumers from unnecessary costs and unethical practices.

Settlement Services and RESPA Compliance

Settlement services play a pivotal role in the real estate transaction process, encompassing a range of activities necessary to complete a property sale, including title searches, appraisals, and legal services. The Real Estate Settlement Procedures Act (RESPA) delineates the framework within which these services operate, aiming to ensure transparency and fairness in the housing market by establishing clear guidelines and prohibitions, particularly concerning referral arrangements.

Title searches are a fundamental component of settlement services, involving a thorough examination of public records to verify the seller's right to transfer ownership and to identify any liens, encumbrances, or claims on the property that could affect the buyer's rights. This process is crucial for the preparation of the title deed, the document that establishes the legal right to own, use, and dispose of property. RESPA mandates that consumers are provided with a choice of title service providers, thereby preventing steering or undue influence by real estate professionals towards specific title companies, which could potentially lead to increased costs for the consumer.

Appraisals are another essential service, providing an objective evaluation of a property's value. Appraisers assess various factors, including the property's condition, location, and comparative market analysis, to determine its fair market value. This valuation plays a critical role in the mortgage lending process, as lenders use the appraised value to determine the loan amount. Under RESPA, lenders are required to provide borrowers with a copy of the appraisal report, ensuring that borrowers are fully informed about the value of their potential investment and the basis for their loan amount.

Legal services in real estate transactions encompass a broad spectrum of activities, including the drafting and review of purchase agreements, the examination of legal titles, and the facilitation of closing procedures. Lawyers ensure that the transaction complies with federal, state, and local laws, safeguarding the interests of both buyers and sellers. RESPA's provisions ensure that consumers have the right to select their own legal representation for real estate transactions, thereby preventing any undue influence or kickbacks for referrals to specific legal professionals.

RESPA explicitly prohibits referral fees and kickbacks among settlement service providers, a practice that could inflate the cost of real estate transactions for consumers. Section 8 of RESPA makes it illegal for any person to give or accept any fee, kickback, or thing of value for the referral of settlement service business. This prohibition extends to any part of a charge for services that are not performed, aiming to eliminate unnecessary costs and ensure that consumers are paying only for legitimate and necessary services associated with the settlement process.

Moreover, RESPA requires the use of a standardized form, the HUD-1 Settlement Statement, to itemize all charges imposed upon borrowers and sellers in connection with the settlement. This requirement facilitates transparency, allowing consumers to review and compare the costs of different settlement services. The act also mandates the provision of the Good Faith Estimate (GFE), enabling borrowers to shop for and compare the prices of settlement services before committing to a particular lender or service provider.

Settlement services are essential to the real estate transaction process, involving various activities that facilitate the legal, fair, and efficient transfer of property. The enforcement of RESPA by the federal government serves to protect consumers from unfair practices and excessive costs through the promotion of transparency, the prohibition of referral fees and kickbacks, and the assurance that borrowers can select their own settlement service providers.

Required Borrower Information (Reg X)

Under Regulation X, which is part of the Real Estate Settlement Procedures Act (RESPA), mortgage loan originators are required to collect specific information from borrowers to initiate the loan application process and to comply with federal disclosure requirements. The collection of this information is critical for the transparency and protection of the borrower, ensuring they are provided with pertinent details about the costs and obligations associated with the mortgage. The six key borrower data points that must be collected to trigger the necessary disclosures are as follows:

1. **Name**: The full legal name of the borrower is essential for identifying the applicant within the loan process. This basic yet crucial piece of information establishes the borrower's identity and is used throughout the loan documentation and verification processes.

2. **Income**: The borrower's income must be accurately reported to assess their ability to repay the loan. This includes all sources of income, such as wages, salaries, commissions, bonuses, and income from investments. The income information helps in calculating the debt-to-income (DTI) ratio, a critical factor in loan underwriting decisions.

3. **Social Security Number (SSN)**: The borrower's SSN is required for a multitude of reasons, including credit checks, tax implications, and as part of the identity verification process. The SSN allows lenders to access the borrower's credit history, which is instrumental in determining creditworthiness and the terms of the loan.

4. **Loan Amount**: The desired loan amount must be specified to give lenders a clear understanding of the borrower's financing needs. This figure helps in determining the loan-to-value (LTV) ratio, another key factor in the underwriting process. The loan amount, combined with the property value, informs the risk assessment and loan structuring.

5. **Property Address**: The physical address of the property to be purchased or refinanced is required. This information is used for appraisal purposes to establish the property's market value, which is necessary for calculating the LTV ratio. Additionally, the property address determines if the property is located in a special flood hazard area, impacting insurance requirements.

6. **Property Value**: An estimate of the property's value must be provided at the time of application. This could be the sales price for a purchase or an estimated value for a refinance. The property value plays a pivotal role in loan structuring, influencing terms such as the need for private mortgage insurance (PMI) and the LTV ratio.

Collecting these six key data points at the outset of the loan application process enables mortgage loan originators to comply with Regulation X by providing timely and accurate disclosures to borrowers. These disclosures, including the Loan Estimate and Closing Disclosure, offer transparency about the loan terms, costs, and the borrower's financial obligations. Compliance with these requirements ensures that borrowers are well-informed and protected in their mortgage transactions, aligning with RESPA's objectives to enhance consumer protection and eliminate abusive practices in the real estate settlement process.

Foreclosure Process and RESPA Obligations

The foreclosure process under the Real Estate Settlement Procedures Act (RESPA) is designed with stringent requirements to ensure that borrowers are afforded every possible opportunity to avoid foreclosure. This process is governed by a framework that mandates servicers to adhere to specific pre-foreclosure notice requirements, engage in loss mitigation efforts, and follow precise timelines for borrower communication. These measures are pivotal in providing protections for homeowners facing financial difficulties and in promoting transparency and fairness within the mortgage servicing industry.

Pre-foreclosure notice requirements are a critical component of the foreclosure process under RESPA. Servicers are obligated to make a good faith effort to contact borrowers who have fallen behind on their mortgage payments before initiating any foreclosure action. This contact should occur no later than 36 days after the borrower becomes delinquent and must continue periodically throughout the delinquency period. The purpose of this early intervention is to inform borrowers of their loss mitigation options and to encourage them to take action that could prevent foreclosure. Additionally, servicers must provide a written notice to the borrower no later than 45 days after the delinquency, outlining the borrower's options to avoid foreclosure, the process for applying for such options, and the contact information for both the servicer and a HUD-approved counseling agency.

Loss mitigation under RESPA involves efforts by servicers to work with delinquent borrowers to avoid foreclosure. These efforts can include loan modifications, forbearance agreements, short sales, or deed-in-lieu of foreclosure agreements. Servicers are required to evaluate the borrower's eligibility for any loss mitigation options promptly, typically within 30 days of receiving a complete loss mitigation application from the borrower. This evaluation must consider all available options and determine which, if any, would allow the borrower to avoid foreclosure. The servicer must then provide the borrower with a notice of decision, detailing the available options or explaining the reasons for denial.

The timelines for borrower communication are meticulously outlined under RESPA. Following the initial contact, servicers must continue to provide delinquent borrowers with periodic statements that include information on loss mitigation options, the foreclosure process, and the borrower's current account status. If the borrower submits a loss mitigation application, the servicer must acknowledge receipt of the application within five business days and inform the borrower if any additional information is required to process the application. Upon making a decision regarding the loss mitigation application, the servicer must inform the borrower in writing of the decision, including the right to appeal if the application is denied, typically within 30 days of receiving a complete application.

Servicer obligations under RESPA are comprehensive and designed to ensure that borrowers are given every opportunity to rectify their delinquent status and retain their homes. Servicers are required to maintain accurate and accessible records of all borrower communications, payments, and loss mitigation efforts. They must also establish and follow fair and impartial procedures for evaluating loss mitigation applications, ensuring that all borrowers are treated equitably. In instances where foreclosure becomes inevitable, servicers must comply with federal, state, and local laws governing the foreclosure process, including providing the borrower with advance notice of foreclosure proceedings.

The foreclosure process under RESPA is structured to balance the interests of both the servicer and the borrower, with a strong emphasis on preventing avoidable foreclosures through early intervention, clear communication, and accessible loss mitigation options. This framework reflects the overarching goal of RESPA to protect homeowners from abusive servicing practices and to promote stability in the housing market.

Initial Escrow Statements Explained

The Real Estate Settlement Procedures Act (RESPA) mandates the provision of initial escrow statements to borrowers as a critical component of the mortgage process, designed to ensure transparency and safeguard consumer interests. This requirement is pivotal in providing borrowers with a clear understanding of the escrow funds that will be collected and disbursed on their behalf for the payment of property taxes, homeowner's insurance, and other charges as applicable. The initial escrow statement serves as a detailed account of the estimated taxes, insurance premiums, and other charges anticipated to be paid from the escrow account during the first year of the loan. It outlines the monthly escrow payment amount, itemizes the charges to be paid from the escrow, and provides an analysis of the escrow account's operation over the course of the year.

Under the provisions of RESPA, lenders are required to deliver this initial escrow statement to borrowers no later than 45 days after the establishment of the escrow account. This timing is crucial as it ensures that borrowers are informed in a timely manner about their escrow payments and the specific use of these funds. The statement must include a projection of the total amount to be paid into the escrow account over the coming year, along with a detailed listing of the expected disbursements from the account for taxes, insurance, and other escrowed items. This projection is based on the lender's best estimates at the time of account setup and may be subject to adjustment based on actual disbursements and changes in tax rates or insurance premiums.

The initial escrow statement also delineates the escrow account's cushion, which is the additional amount lenders are allowed to collect to cover unforeseen disbursements or increases in the costs of taxes or insurance. RESPA permits lenders to maintain a cushion equivalent to two months of escrow payments, a regulation designed to prevent significant shortfalls in the escrow account that could impact the lender's ability to make payments on behalf of the borrower. However, the act strictly limits this cushion to ensure that borrowers are not unduly burdened with excessive escrow collections.

Furthermore, the initial escrow statement plays a vital role in ensuring that borrowers are adequately informed about their rights and responsibilities related to the escrow account. It must include information on how the borrower can question the accuracy of the statement and the procedures for addressing any concerns or discrepancies. This aspect of the initial escrow statement is essential for empowering borrowers to take an active role in managing their escrow accounts and ensuring that they are being charged accurately for taxes and insurance.

In addition to the initial escrow statement, RESPA requires that borrowers receive an annual escrow statement each year, providing a review of the account's activity and adjustments to the monthly escrow payment as necessary based on actual disbursements and changes in tax or insurance costs. This annual statement ensures ongoing transparency and allows for the reconciliation of the escrow account, ensuring that it accurately reflects the borrower's actual expenses for taxes and insurance.

The initial and annual escrow statements are fundamental components of the protections afforded to consumers under RESPA, designed to ensure clarity, transparency, and fairness in the handling of escrow accounts. By requiring these disclosures, RESPA helps to safeguard borrowers from unexpected increases in their monthly mortgage payments due to escrow shortages and provides a mechanism for borrowers to understand and manage their escrow payments effectively.

Equal Credit Opportunity Act (ECOA)

ECOA Permissible Lender Actions

Under the Equal Credit Opportunity Act (ECOA), lenders are granted the authority to undertake a variety of actions to assess a borrower's creditworthiness and financial stability. This is crucial for making informed lending decisions while simultaneously adhering to strict anti-discrimination laws. The permissible acts under ECOA are designed to ensure that all applicants are evaluated based on their financial merits, without regard to race, color, religion, national origin, sex, marital status, age, or because all or part of an applicant's income derives from any public assistance program.

Evaluating Creditworthiness: Lenders are permitted to request detailed financial information from applicants. This includes, but is not limited to, income level, employment history, credit scores, credit reports, existing debts, and assets. This evaluation process is fundamental to determining the likelihood that the borrower will fulfill their loan obligations. Lenders use this information to calculate key financial ratios such as the debt-to-income (DTI) ratio and the loan-to-value (LTV) ratio, which are critical indicators of financial health and risk.

Financial Stability Assessment: Beyond credit scores and income, lenders are also allowed to consider the stability and consistency of an applicant's income and employment. This can involve analyzing the length of time an individual has been with their current employer or the consistency of income over a period of years. Such assessments help lenders gauge the reliability of the income, which is a significant factor in ensuring loan repayment.

Use of Credit Reports: The ECOA permits lenders to obtain and use credit reports from recognized credit bureaus to evaluate an applicant's credit history. This includes looking at past loan repayments, credit utilization, and any instances of bankruptcy or defaults. The act ensures that lenders have access to comprehensive credit information, enabling a thorough assessment of credit risk.

Anti-Discrimination Measures: While evaluating creditworthiness and financial stability, lenders must strictly adhere to ECOA's anti-discrimination provisions. This means decisions cannot be based on any of the protected characteristics. For instance, a lender cannot refuse a loan or offer less favorable terms based solely on an applicant's race or the fact that their income comes from public assistance programs.

Joint Credit: Under ECOA, lenders are allowed to ask about marital status and to offer joint credit to married couples or co-applicants. This permits lenders to consider the combined financial information of the applicants, which can be particularly relevant in assessing the overall creditworthiness for a joint loan.

Age Consideration: While ECOA protects applicants from discrimination based on age, lenders are permitted to consider age in certain contexts. For example, a lender can use age to determine the meaning of other factors important for creditworthiness. This might include considerations about whether a borrower is of legal age to enter into a contract or assessing the likelihood of continued income in retirement.

The ECOA establishes a framework that allows lenders to perform comprehensive evaluations of applicants' financial situations, ensuring decisions are made fairly and based on relevant financial criteria. This framework supports the dual goals of facilitating access to credit for consumers while allowing lenders to manage risk effectively.

Prohibited Discrimination Factors

In the realm of mortgage lending, the Equal Credit Opportunity Act (ECOA) plays a pivotal role in ensuring that all applicants are afforded an equal opportunity to secure financing, free from discrimination based on non-financial factors. The ECOA delineates specific categories under which lenders cannot discriminate, thereby fostering a more inclusive and equitable lending environment. These prohibited factors include race, color, religion, national origin, sex, marital status, age, and the receipt of income from public assistance programs.

Race and color stand as fundamental attributes of an individual's identity, and the ECOA explicitly prohibits lenders from considering these factors in the evaluation process. This prohibition ensures that applicants are judged solely on their financial merits rather than prejudicial biases. Similarly, religion and national origin are also protected categories, safeguarding applicants from being unfavorably judged based on their cultural, geographical, or spiritual backgrounds.

Sex and marital status are additional dimensions where the ECOA mandates impartiality. Decisions regarding loan approval, terms, and conditions must be made without regard to whether an applicant is male, female, married, single, divorced, or widowed. This ensures that gender or marital dynamics do not influence the lending process, promoting fairness and equality.

Age is another critical factor where discrimination is expressly forbidden, with a specific provision that protects applicants aged 62 and older. However, the ECOA does allow for age to be considered insofar as it pertains to the legality of entering into a contract or the assessment of income stability over time. For instance, lenders may evaluate whether an applicant's income, potentially derived from retirement benefits, is likely to continue for the foreseeable future, ensuring the ability to repay the loan.

Income source, particularly from public assistance programs such as Social Security, disability, or unemployment benefits, is also protected under the ECOA. Lenders are required to treat income from these sources the same as income from employment, investments, or other sources, provided it is reliable and likely to continue. This provision ensures that applicants are not penalized for the source of their income, as long as it is legitimate and verifiable.

The ECOA's prohibitions on discrimination are not merely ethical guidelines but enforceable legal standards that lenders must adhere to. Compliance with these standards is monitored and enforced by regulatory bodies, including the Consumer Financial Protection Bureau (CFPB), ensuring that lenders implement fair lending practices. Violations of the ECOA can result in significant legal and financial consequences for lenders, underscoring the importance of rigorous adherence to these anti-discrimination measures.

In practice, adherence to the ECOA's provisions requires lenders to establish and maintain lending policies and practices that are both fair and transparent. This includes training for loan officers and underwriters on the importance of evaluating applications based on financial criteria alone, without regard to any of the prohibited discriminatory factors. Additionally, lenders must ensure that their marketing practices do not target or exclude potential applicants based on these protected characteristics, further reinforcing the principle of equal access to credit.

The ECOA's role in eliminating discrimination in the lending process is a critical component of a broader societal commitment to fairness and equality. By strictly prohibiting discrimination based on race, color, religion, national origin, sex, marital status, age, or public assistance income, the ECOA helps to ensure that all individuals have an equal opportunity to obtain mortgage financing based on their financial qualifications, contributing to a more inclusive and equitable financial ecosystem.

Loan Denial: Valid Reasons

In the context of mortgage loan origination under the Equal Credit Opportunity Act (ECOA), lenders are tasked with a comprehensive evaluation of an applicant's financial health to determine their eligibility for a loan. This evaluation process is critical to ensuring that loans are granted to individuals who are likely to fulfill their repayment obligations. Despite the stringent anti-discrimination laws that mandate fairness and equality in the lending process, there are legitimate financial reasons why a loan application might be denied. These reasons are rooted in the lender's obligation to assess risk and ensure that the borrower has the financial capacity to repay the loan.

Insufficient Income: One of the primary reasons for loan denial is insufficient income. Lenders meticulously analyze an applicant's income to ensure it is stable, reliable, and sufficient to cover monthly loan payments in addition to existing financial obligations. This analysis often involves calculating the debt-to-income (DTI) ratio, which is a critical financial metric used to gauge an applicant's ability to manage monthly payments. A high DTI ratio indicates that an individual's debt payments consume a significant portion of their income, which can lead to loan denial due to the increased risk of default.

Poor Credit History: An applicant's credit history is a detailed record of their past borrowing and repayment activities, including any late payments, defaults, bankruptcies, or foreclosures. A poor credit history suggests a pattern of financial irresponsibility or an inability to manage debt effectively. Lenders rely on credit scores, which are derived from credit histories, to assess an applicant's creditworthiness. Low credit scores can result in loan denial, as they reflect a higher likelihood of future defaults.

Excessive Debt: Apart from evaluating income, lenders also review an applicant's existing debt obligations. This includes all outstanding debts such as car loans, credit card debt, student loans, and other personal loans. Excessive debt, even with sufficient income, can be a cause for concern for lenders. It raises questions about the borrower's ability to take on additional financial burdens without compromising their ability to make consistent loan payments. The presence of excessive debt can lead to a loan application being denied due to the perceived increase in default risk.

Inability to Meet Repayment Obligations: Ultimately, the decision to approve or deny a loan hinges on the lender's confidence in the applicant's ability to meet repayment obligations. This encompasses more than just the ability to make monthly payments; it also includes the borrower's overall financial stability, the predictability of their income, and their capacity to handle unforeseen financial challenges. Factors such as employment instability, irregular income, or a lack of financial reserves can contribute to a lender's decision to deny a loan, as these issues signal a higher risk of payment interruptions or default.

Lenders are required to provide applicants with a Notice of Adverse Action when a loan application is denied, which must include specific reasons for the denial. This transparency ensures that applicants understand the factors that influenced the decision and provides them with an opportunity to address these issues before reapplying for a loan in the future.

The evaluation of an applicant's financial situation is a complex process that involves a careful balance between ensuring access to credit and managing lending risk. While the ECOA provides a framework for fair and equitable lending practices, it also recognizes the necessity of basing loan approval decisions on sound financial criteria. By adhering to these principles, lenders can contribute to a stable and responsible mortgage lending environment.

Regulation B: Lender Obligations Under ECOA

Regulation B, formally known as 12 CFR Part 1002, operationalizes the Equal Credit Opportunity Act (ECOA) by delineating the obligations lenders must adhere to in order to prevent discrimination in the credit process. This regulation is pivotal in ensuring that all consumers have equitable access to credit, irrespective of race, color, religion, national origin, sex, marital status, age, or receipt of income from public assistance programs.

Lender Obligations under Regulation B are multifaceted, focusing on non-discrimination, notification requirements, and information retention. Firstly, lenders are prohibited from discriminating against applicants on the basis of protected characteristics. This includes making any decision regarding creditworthiness based on these factors or considering the race, sex, or age of a person in any aspect of a credit transaction that could influence the outcome negatively against the protected class.

Notification Requirements mandate that lenders must promptly inform applicants of the action taken on their credit applications. This must occur within 30 days of receiving a completed application. If an application is denied, lenders are required to provide a notice of adverse action, detailing the specific reasons for the denial or the right of the applicant to request such reasons within 60 days. This transparency is crucial for applicants to understand the decision-making process and provides an opportunity to rectify any inaccuracies or to improve their financial standing for future applications.

Information Retention is another critical aspect of Regulation B, requiring lenders to maintain records of all credit applications for a period of 25 months after notifying applicants of the action taken on their applications. This retention policy facilitates the enforcement of ECOA by allowing regulatory bodies to review lender compliance with the law. For applications that result in an unfavorable action for the applicant, such as a denial, the lender must also retain records that demonstrate the criteria used in making the credit decision, ensuring that these decisions can be audited for compliance with anti-discrimination laws.

Regulation B also addresses the **collection of applicant information**, stipulating that lenders may inquire about certain personal information, such as marital status and dependents, for the purpose of ascertaining creditworthiness, provided that the information is collected in a manner consistent with ECOA's anti-discrimination objectives. However, it places strict limitations on how this information can be used in the credit evaluation process. For instance, income derived from alimony or child support can only be considered if the applicant chooses to disclose it, acknowledging its reliability and likelihood of continuance.

Furthermore, Regulation B outlines the **use of evaluation systems**, such as credit scoring models, ensuring they are empirically derived, demonstrably and statistically sound, and not based on any prohibited basis. Lenders are encouraged to regularly review their credit criteria and the application of such systems to ensure they do not inadvertently discriminate against any applicant.

In essence, Regulation B serves as a comprehensive framework for fair lending practices, emphasizing the importance of equitable treatment in the credit industry. By adhering to these guidelines, lenders not only comply with federal law but also contribute to a more inclusive financial ecosystem, where credit decisions are made based on merit rather than personal characteristics.

Notifying Borrowers of Credit Decisions

Under the Equal Credit Opportunity Act (ECOA), lenders are mandated to notify borrowers of the credit decision within a specific timeframe. This obligation ensures transparency and fairness in the lending process, providing applicants with timely information about the outcome of their loan application. The regulation stipulates that lenders must send a notification of action taken on a credit application within **30 days** after receiving a completed application from the borrower. This critical timeframe plays a significant role in maintaining an efficient credit system, allowing applicants to quickly understand their credit status and, if necessary, seek alternatives or address any issues that led to a denial.

The notification requirement under ECOA serves multiple purposes. Primarily, it ensures that applicants are not left in the dark about the status of their loan applications, fostering a sense of trust and accountability in the financial system. Furthermore, in cases where the application is denied, the lender must provide a **Notice of Adverse Action**, which includes specific reasons for the denial. This notice is crucial as it must detail the particular factors that influenced the decision, offering the applicant an opportunity to rectify any discrepancies or improve their financial standing for future applications.

The **Notice of Adverse Action** is not merely a formality but a document enriched with information that empowers the borrower. It must clearly articulate the reasons for denial, such as insufficient income, high debt-to-income ratio, or poor credit history, among others. Additionally, it should inform the applicant of their right to obtain a copy of the credit report that was used in making the decision, free of charge, if requested within 60 days. This aspect of the notification process underscores the lender's obligation to provide actionable feedback, rather than a mere rejection.

Lenders must meticulously adhere to the 30-day notification rule, as failure to comply can result in regulatory penalties and damage to the lender's reputation. Compliance with this rule is monitored by regulatory bodies, including the Consumer Financial Protection Bureau (CFPB), ensuring that lenders uphold the standards set forth by ECOA. The 30-day period is calculated from the date the lender receives the completed application, which underscores the importance of lenders maintaining accurate records of application dates and decision timelines.

In the context of ensuring compliance and fostering positive borrower-lender relationships, lenders may adopt automated systems to track application dates and ensure timely decision notifications. These systems can help prevent oversights and ensure that all applicants receive their notifications within the mandated timeframe, thereby upholding the principles of fairness and transparency in the lending process.

The requirement to notify borrowers of credit decisions within 30 days reflects the broader objectives of ECOA to eliminate discrimination and promote equal access to credit. By mandating timely communication, the regulation ensures that all applicants, regardless of their background, are afforded a fair and transparent evaluation process. This aspect of ECOA is integral to building a more inclusive financial environment where decisions are made based on objective criteria, and applicants are provided with the information needed to understand and potentially improve their financial health.

Required Disclosures for Denied Applications

Upon the denial of a loan application, lenders are mandated under the Equal Credit Opportunity Act (ECOA) to issue a **Notice of Adverse Action** to the applicant. This notice serves a critical function in the lending process by informing the applicant of the specific reasons for the loan application's denial. The timing of this notice is crucial; lenders must provide it within **30 days** following the decision to deny the application. This prompt notification allows applicants to understand the factors contributing to the denial and, if possible, take steps to address these issues before submitting future loan applications.

The **Notice of Adverse Action** must include several key pieces of information to comply with ECOA regulations. Firstly, it should clearly state the specific reasons for the loan denial. Reasons might include insufficient income for the requested loan amount, a high debt-to-income ratio, or a poor credit history. These reasons must be explicitly detailed in the notice to provide the applicant with a clear understanding of the decision. Vague or generic explanations, such as "you did not meet our minimum criteria," are not acceptable under ECOA guidelines. Instead, the notice should provide actionable feedback that the applicant can use to improve their financial standing or correct any inaccuracies in their credit report.

Additionally, the notice must inform the applicant of their right to obtain a copy of the credit report that was used in the decision-making process. This right is critical, as it allows applicants to verify the accuracy of the credit information that influenced the lender's decision. If the applicant requests this report within **60 days** of receiving the Notice of Adverse Action, they are entitled to receive it free of charge. This provision ensures transparency in the lending process and provides an avenue for applicants to dispute any incorrect information contained in their credit report.

Furthermore, the notice should inform the applicant of their right to dispute the accuracy or completeness of any information provided by the credit reporting agency. This is an essential aspect of consumer rights under the Fair Credit Reporting Act (FCRA), which works in tandem with ECOA to protect applicants from inaccuracies in credit reporting that could unfairly impact their ability to obtain credit.

Lenders must also disclose the name, address, and phone number of the credit reporting agency that supplied the credit report. This information is necessary for applicants who wish to contact the agency directly to obtain their credit report or dispute inaccuracies. Providing this contact information facilitates the process for applicants to engage with credit reporting agencies and exercise their rights under the FCRA.

The **Notice of Adverse Action** is a fundamental component of the loan application process, designed to ensure fairness and transparency in lending decisions. By providing specific reasons for loan denial, informing applicants of their rights regarding credit reports, and facilitating the dispute of inaccuracies, this notice empowers applicants to take proactive steps towards securing credit in the future. Compliance with the timing and content requirements of the notice is not only a legal obligation for lenders under ECOA but also a critical practice in maintaining trust and integrity in the lending process.

Adverse Action: Definition and Notifications

Adverse action in the context of the Equal Credit Opportunity Act (ECOA) refers to any action taken by a lender that is unfavorable to the interests of an applicant or existing borrower. This can include the denial of credit, offering credit at terms less favorable than those requested, or modifying or terminating existing credit unfavorably. Examples of adverse actions include denying a mortgage application, offering a higher interest rate than applied for, reducing a credit limit, or refusing to approve a loan modification.

Under ECOA, lenders are required to provide a notice of adverse action to applicants whose requests for credit are denied or who receive less favorable terms than those for which they applied. This notice must include specific reasons for the decision or state that the applicant has the right to request the reasons within 60 days. The notice must be provided within 30 days of the lender's decision.

The adverse action notice serves several important purposes. It informs the applicant of the decision and provides transparency about the reasons behind it, which can help the applicant understand areas of their financial profile that may need improvement. It also ensures that lenders are held accountable for their credit decision processes, promoting fairness and nondiscrimination in lending practices.

The reasons for adverse action must be specific and cannot be vague or generic. For example, stating that an application was denied due to "insufficient income" is not sufficient without explaining what aspect of the income was inadequate. Common reasons for adverse action include high debt-to-income ratio, insufficient credit history, or low credit score.

Lenders must also inform the applicant of their right to obtain a free credit report if the decision was based in whole or in part on information contained in the report. This must be done within 60 days of receiving the applicant's request for the reasons behind the adverse action.

It's crucial for mortgage loan originators and lenders to understand and comply with the notification rules regarding adverse actions to avoid regulatory penalties and to maintain trust and transparency with applicants. Compliance with these rules also supports the broader objectives of ECOA in preventing discrimination and promoting fair access to credit.

Application Data & ECOA's Elderly Definition

When completing a mortgage application under the Equal Credit Opportunity Act (ECOA), lenders are mandated to collect certain pieces of information from applicants to comply with federal regulations and to make informed lending decisions. The mandatory application data includes, but is not limited to, the borrower's name, income, social security number (SSN), estimated value of the property, loan amount sought, and the address of the property to be mortgaged. This information forms the basis of the lender's assessment of the borrower's creditworthiness and ability to repay the loan.

Under the provisions of ECOA, age is considered a protected category. Specifically, the act defines the term **"elderly"** as any person aged **62 years or older**. This definition is critical for mortgage loan originators and lenders to understand, as it prohibits discrimination based on age in all aspects of the credit transaction process. It ensures that older applicants are not unfairly denied credit or offered less favorable terms simply because of their age.

The legal implications of age as a protected category under ECOA are significant. Lenders must exercise caution to not only avoid explicit discrimination but also to prevent practices that could have a disparate impact on elderly applicants. For instance, overly stringent income verification processes that do not consider retirement income as stable and ongoing could be deemed discriminatory. Lenders are encouraged to consider all sources of an applicant's income, including pensions, Social Security benefits, and other retirement funds, in their income assessment processes.

Furthermore, ECOA mandates that lenders make credit decisions based on reliable measures of creditworthiness, not on assumptions or stereotypes about certain groups, including the elderly. This means that all applicants, regardless of age, must be evaluated based on their actual financial information and credit history.

In practice, compliance with ECOA's provisions regarding the elderly requires lenders to implement policies and training programs that ensure all employees understand how to properly process applications from older individuals. This includes recognizing the various types of income that are common among retirees and understanding the legal protections afforded to the elderly under federal law.

Lenders found in violation of ECOA, including its provisions related to age discrimination, can face significant legal and financial consequences. Regulatory agencies, including the Consumer Financial Protection Bureau (CFPB), actively enforce ECOA's requirements, and lenders may be subject to penalties, required to make restitution to affected borrowers, or both.

The definition of elderly as individuals aged 62 years or older under ECOA highlights the significance of fair lending practices and the necessity for mortgage professionals to ensure that all applicants receive equitable treatment, free from age-related bias. Adhering to these regulations not only safeguards consumers but also maintains the integrity of the lending process.

MLO Reporting When Borrower Declines Info

In compliance with the Equal Credit Opportunity Act (ECOA), Mortgage Loan Originators (MLOs) are tasked with ensuring that all applications for credit are processed without discrimination based on race, color, religion, national origin, sex, marital status, age, or any other protected status. This includes the collection of demographic information, which is used for monitoring purposes under the Home Mortgage Disclosure Act (HMDA). However, situations may arise where a borrower opts not to provide information regarding their race or gender on the loan application. In such instances, the MLO is required to navigate this scenario with care, adhering to specific regulatory guidelines designed to uphold the integrity of the lending process while respecting the applicant's preferences.

When a borrower declines to self-report their race or gender, the MLO must then report this information based on visual observation or surname, as per the regulatory requirements set forth by the Federal Financial Institutions Examination Council (FFIEC). This approach is part of a broader effort to ensure the collection of demographic data, which plays a critical role in identifying potential patterns of discrimination within the lending industry. The process for reporting based on visual observation or surname is outlined in detail within the HMDA guidelines, which provide a structured framework for MLOs to follow.

Visual Observation: If the application is taken in person, and the borrower chooses not to disclose their race or gender, the MLO is required to make a determination based on visual observation. This involves the MLO using their judgment to select the race and gender categories that they believe best fit the applicant. It is crucial that MLOs approach this process with a high degree of professionalism and sensitivity, recognizing the potential for biases and the importance of making an objective assessment to the best of their ability.

Surname Analysis: In cases where the loan application is not taken in person (e.g., online or over the phone) and the borrower does not provide their race or gender, the MLO may use the applicant's surname to infer this information. This method relies on databases and resources that associate surnames with particular racial or ethnic groups. While not as direct as visual observation, surname analysis provides an alternative means of reporting demographic information when direct observation is not possible.

It is important to note that the requirement for MLOs to report race and gender based on visual observation or surname does not supersede the borrower's right to privacy or the principles of fair lending. Rather, it serves as a mechanism to fulfill regulatory requirements aimed at promoting transparency and fairness in the mortgage lending process. MLOs must ensure that their actions are in strict compliance with ECOA and HMDA regulations, documenting their methodology and the basis for any determination made in the absence of self-reported information by the borrower.

Furthermore, MLOs and lending institutions are encouraged to provide clear explanations to borrowers about the purpose of collecting demographic information and the regulatory obligations that necessitate the reporting of race and gender, even when self-disclosure is not provided. By fostering an environment of transparency and trust, MLOs can navigate the sensitive aspects of demographic reporting while maintaining the confidentiality and respect due to all applicants.

The requirement for MLOs to report race and gender based on visual observation or surname when a borrower chooses not to self-report is an essential aspect of the regulatory framework that governs fair lending practices. MLOs are expected to demonstrate diligence, sensitivity, and strict adherence to established guidelines while fulfilling this obligation. This ensures that the collection of demographic data is performed in a way that honors borrower preferences and supports the overarching objectives of fairness and equality within the lending industry.

Co-signer Requirements Explained

Under the Equal Credit Opportunity Act (ECOA), the inclusion of a co-signer in a mortgage application process is subject to specific regulatory requirements aimed at ensuring fair treatment and nondiscrimination. A co-signer, by definition, is an individual who agrees to take on the financial responsibility of the mortgage payments should the primary borrower fail to make payments. This section delineates the valid requirements for co-signers and underscores the importance of equal treatment, emphasizing that co-signers cannot be mandated based on protected categories such as race, color, religion, national origin, sex, marital status, age, or receipt of income from public assistance programs.

Valid Co-signer Requirements: For a co-signer to be considered valid under ECOA, they must have sufficient income and creditworthiness to satisfy the lender's criteria for loan approval. This includes a stable income source, a satisfactory credit score, and a debt-to-income ratio that falls within the lender's permissible range. The co-signer's financial health is scrutinized to ensure they can feasibly assume the loan's obligations if necessary. Importantly, the primary borrower and the co-signer are jointly responsible for the loan, and this shared liability must be clearly communicated and understood by all parties involved.

Ensuring Equal Treatment: The ECOA mandates that all applicants, including co-signers, must be evaluated based on their financial credentials without bias or discrimination. Lenders are prohibited from imposing different terms or conditions on a loan based on any of the protected categories. This principle of equal treatment extends to the solicitation and acceptance of co-signers. For instance, a lender cannot require a co-signer for one applicant based on age if the same requirement is not uniformly applied to all applicants under similar financial circumstances.

Prohibition Against Mandatory Co-signers Based on Protected Categories: It is critical to note that lenders cannot mandate the inclusion of a co-signer solely because an applicant falls within a protected category. For example, suggesting or requiring a co-signer because an applicant is elderly or because of the applicant's national origin violates ECOA's anti-discrimination provisions. Any decision regarding the necessity of a co-signer must be strictly grounded in the financial information and creditworthiness of the applicant, not on assumptions or stereotypes associated with any protected characteristics.

Documentation and Disclosure: When a co-signer is involved in a loan application, lenders must adhere to strict documentation and disclosure requirements. This includes providing all parties with accurate information regarding their rights and obligations. The co-signer must receive the same loan disclosures as the primary borrower, ensuring transparency about the loan terms, interest rates, and potential risks.

Compliance and Oversight: Lenders must maintain rigorous compliance protocols to monitor and enforce adherence to ECOA requirements concerning co-signers. This includes training for loan officers and underwriters on the proper evaluation of co-signers and the importance of avoiding discriminatory practices. Regulatory bodies, such as the Consumer Financial Protection Bureau (CFPB), oversee lender activities to ensure compliance with ECOA, and violations can result in significant penalties, including fines and corrective actions.

In essence, the role of a co-signer in the mortgage application process is governed by principles of fairness and nondiscrimination. By adhering to ECOA's requirements, lenders and mortgage loan originators not only uphold the law but also contribute to a lending environment that respects the dignity and financial aspirations of all individuals, regardless of their background or life circumstances.

Acceptable Income for Loan Review

In assessing a borrower's ability to repay a mortgage loan, lenders consider various sources of income under the guidelines set forth by the Equal Credit Opportunity Act (ECOA). It is crucial for mortgage loan originators (MLOs) to understand what constitutes acceptable income to ensure compliance with federal regulations and to facilitate fair lending practices. Acceptable income sources must be **consistent, verifiable, and likely to continue**. This section delves into the types of income that meet these criteria.

Salary and Wages: The most straightforward source of income, salary and wages from employment, are considered stable and verifiable through pay stubs, W-2 forms, and employer verification. Lenders look for a history of steady employment, typically two years in the same job or field, to deem this income reliable.

Self-Employment Income: Income from self-employment is acceptable but requires more documentation for verification due to its potentially variable nature. Tax returns, profit and loss statements, and business bank statements over two years are commonly used to establish the stability and continuity of self-employment income. Lenders may also consider the viability and financial health of the business.

Public Assistance Income: Benefits received from public assistance programs can be included as part of a borrower's income if they are expected to continue for at least three years from the date of the mortgage application. Documentation from the providing agency confirming benefit amounts and duration is necessary for verification.

Alimony or Child Support: Income received from alimony or child support may be considered if the borrower chooses to disclose it and can prove that it is consistent and likely to continue. Court orders, separation agreements, and a history of payment receipts are required to verify these income sources. It is important to note that under ECOA, borrowers cannot be compelled to disclose alimony or child support income if they do not wish to rely on it for loan qualification.

Other Considerations for Acceptable Income:
- The income must not only be verifiable but also stable. Lenders typically look for income that has been consistently received for the past two years and is expected to continue.
- The predictability of income is also assessed. For instance, bonuses, commissions, and overtime may be considered if they are shown to be regular and recurring.
- Lenders will evaluate the likelihood of continued income based on the borrower's occupation, employer stability, and industry trends.

In conclusion, understanding the nuances of what constitutes acceptable income for loan review is essential for MLOs. This knowledge ensures that borrowers are evaluated fairly based on their ability to repay the loan, in line with ECOA guidelines. Proper documentation and thorough verification of income sources are key components of the loan application process, supporting the principles of responsible lending and equal opportunity.

Creditworthiness Factors

Assessing a borrower's creditworthiness is a multifaceted process that hinges on several critical factors, each playing a pivotal role in determining the likelihood of loan repayment. These factors—credit history, income stability, employment history, and the debt-to-income (DTI) ratio—are essential in the evaluation process under the guidelines of the Equal Credit Opportunity Act (ECOA). This act ensures that all borrowers are assessed based on objective, non-discriminatory criteria, fostering a fair lending environment.

Credit history stands as one of the primary indicators of a borrower's financial reliability. It encompasses a record of the borrower's previous loan repayments, credit card usage, and any defaults or bankruptcies. Lenders scrutinize credit reports to gauge a borrower's financial behavior, including payment punctuality, the length of credit history, types of credit used, and the frequency of credit applications. A robust credit history, marked by timely payments and a diverse credit mix, significantly enhances a borrower's creditworthiness.

Income stability is another cornerstone of credit evaluation. Lenders seek assurance that the borrower has a reliable, steady income source sufficient to cover loan repayments, in addition to other living expenses. This evaluation often requires borrowers to provide proof of income, such as pay stubs, tax returns, and employer verification letters. For self-employed individuals or those with variable incomes, lenders may require additional documentation to establish a consistent income pattern over several years.

Employment history further contributes to the assessment of creditworthiness. A stable employment record, typically spanning two years or more with the same employer or in the same industry, suggests financial stability and predictability, making the borrower a lower risk. Lenders may verify employment history through direct contact with employers, review of income documents, or both. Frequent job changes or periods of unemployment may raise concerns about the borrower's ability to maintain steady income for loan repayment.

The debt-to-income (DTI) ratio is a critical metric that compares a borrower's total monthly debt payments to their gross monthly income. It provides lenders with a direct insight into the borrower's financial obligations relative to their income, offering a clear picture of their capacity to take on and repay new debt. A lower DTI ratio indicates a healthier balance between debt and income, enhancing the borrower's creditworthiness. Lenders typically prefer a DTI ratio of 43% or lower, as higher ratios may signal financial strain and an increased risk of default.

In the context of the ECOA, it is paramount for lenders to apply these criteria uniformly across all applicants, ensuring that assessments of creditworthiness are based solely on financial factors without regard to race, color, religion, national origin, sex, marital status, age, or any other protected characteristic. This objective, data-driven approach not only upholds the principles of fair lending but also supports the financial integrity of the lending process, ensuring that loans are granted to borrowers who demonstrate a strong capacity for repayment.

Truth in Lending Act (TILA)

Purpose of TILA

The Truth in Lending Act (TILA), enacted in 1968, serves as a cornerstone in the regulation of the United States' lending environment, specifically targeting the necessity for lenders to disclose credit terms in a clear and standardized manner to consumers. At its core, TILA aims to equip borrowers with the information necessary to make informed credit decisions, fostering a transparent lending atmosphere that benefits both lenders and consumers alike. This legislation mandates that lenders disclose critical information about the cost of credit, including the annual percentage rate (APR), term of the loan, and total costs to the borrower, in a precise and understandable format before any agreement is signed.

TILA's significance in promoting informed credit decisions cannot be overstated. By requiring lenders to present details of the credit offer in a standardized format, TILA ensures that consumers can compare different credit offers on a like-for-like basis. This comparison is crucial for consumers to understand the long-term implications of their credit choices, including how interest rates and finance charges can affect the total amount they will pay over the life of the loan. The act's requirements help prevent the concealment of fees and the understatement of the cost of borrowing, which are practices that can lead to consumers inadvertently committing to credit terms that are unfavorable or beyond their financial means.

Furthermore, TILA standardizes cost disclosures through detailed regulations that dictate how lenders must calculate and present the APR. This standardization is vital because the APR encompasses not just the interest rate but also other charges and fees associated with the loan, providing a more comprehensive picture of the loan's cost. The APR calculation and disclosure requirements ensure that borrowers receive a fuller understanding of their financial obligations, enabling them to make choices that align with their financial goals and capabilities.

Transparency in credit terms and lending practices is another cornerstone of TILA. The act mandates that lenders provide borrowers with clear and timely disclosures about the terms of their credit agreement, including information on the right to rescind certain types of credit transactions within a three-day period. This transparency is instrumental in preventing misunderstandings and disputes between borrowers and lenders, thereby fostering trust in the financial marketplace. It also empowers consumers to exercise their rights effectively, including the right to cancel a loan agreement within the stipulated period if they decide that the terms are not in their best interest.

In essence, TILA plays a pivotal role in ensuring that the lending market functions efficiently and ethically. By requiring the disclosure of critical information in a standardized format, TILA protects consumers from deceptive and predatory lending practices, supports competitive market conditions, and promotes the responsible use of credit. Its ongoing relevance is reflected in the periodic updates and amendments it has received to address emerging lending practices and financial products, ensuring that its protections evolve in line with the changing dynamics of the credit market. Through these mechanisms, TILA significantly contributes to the broader objective of safeguarding consumer rights while enhancing the integrity and stability of the financial system.

Loans Covered Under TILA

The Truth in Lending Act (TILA) encompasses a wide array of loan types, primarily focusing on consumer-purpose loans which are extended for personal, family, or household purposes. This includes both open-end credit, such as credit cards and home equity lines of credit (HELOCs), and closed-end credit, which refers to more traditional loans where the borrower receives the entire loan amount upfront and repays it over a specified period. Open-end credit offers a revolving line of credit with a limit that can be utilized, repaid, and then used again, providing flexibility for the borrower to manage their financial needs over time. Closed-end credit, on the other hand, is typically associated with specific lending purposes like purchasing a home or a car, with set payment schedules and interest rates.

TILA mandates that lenders disclose critical terms and costs associated with these loans, ensuring borrowers are fully informed about their financial obligations. The act's disclosure requirements are designed to facilitate comparisons between different lending options, empowering consumers to make decisions that best suit their financial situations. For example, lenders must provide clear information about the annual percentage rate (APR), finance charges, the total amount financed, and the payment schedule for closed-end credit loans. For open-end credit, disclosures include the APR, fees, and other charges, providing a comprehensive overview of the costs involved.

However, not all loans fall under TILA's purview. Exemptions include loans made for business, commercial, or agricultural purposes, which are not considered consumer-purpose loans and thus are not subject to the same disclosure requirements. This distinction is crucial for lenders and borrowers alike, as it delineates the scope of TILA's protections and ensures that its provisions are targeted towards consumer transactions. The rationale behind these exemptions lies in the premise that business or commercial loans are entered into by individuals or entities with a greater understanding or capacity to engage in such transactions, potentially negating the need for the detailed consumer protections TILA provides.

Furthermore, TILA does not apply to loans extended by a creditor who makes five or fewer mortgages in a calendar year, thereby exempting certain private lenders and small-scale financiers from its requirements. This exemption is designed to balance the need for consumer protection with the recognition that not all lenders operate on a scale where the full scope of TILA's provisions would be practical or necessary.

Understanding the loans covered under TILA, along with its exemptions, is essential for both lenders and borrowers to navigate the regulatory landscape effectively. Lenders must ensure compliance with TILA's disclosure requirements for eligible loans, while borrowers benefit from the protections and transparency it affords, enabling them to make informed decisions about their credit options. The act's focus on consumer-purpose loans underscores its role in safeguarding consumer interests, highlighting the importance of clear, comprehensive financial disclosures in the lending process.

Key Terms: APR, Finance Charge, Dwelling, Loan

Understanding the key terms associated with the Truth in Lending Act (TILA) is essential for mortgage loan originators and those involved in the real estate finance sector. These terms not only help in navigating the complexities of mortgage transactions but also ensure compliance with federal regulations, thereby safeguarding both the lender and the borrower.

The Annual Percentage Rate (APR) is a critical term under TILA, representing the cost of credit expressed as a yearly rate. Unlike the nominal interest rate, the APR includes any fees or additional costs associated with the loan, making it a more comprehensive measure of the loan's cost. The APR is calculated using a complex formula that takes into account the nominal interest rate, any charges or fees, and the term of the loan. The formula for calculating APR can be represented as:

$$APR = \left(\frac{P}{A}\right) \times \left(\frac{365}{n}\right) \times 100$$

where P is the total amount of interest paid over the course of the year, A is the amount of the loan outstanding, and n is the number of days in the loan term. This calculation ensures that borrowers can compare different loan offers on an apples-to-apples basis, understanding the true cost of borrowing beyond just the interest rate.

The finance charge is another pivotal term, encompassing all costs, in the form of fees, interest, or loan charges, paid by the borrower over the loan's life, excluding the actual loan amount. It's a broad term that includes origination fees, transaction fees, and any charge payable directly or indirectly by the borrower and imposed directly or indirectly by the lender as an incident to or a condition of the extension of credit. Thus, the finance charge is a critical figure that affects the overall cost of the loan and, consequently, the APR.

A dwelling, in the context of TILA, refers to a residential structure that includes houses, condominiums, apartments, and similar places of residence. The act's protections apply to loans secured by a dwelling, emphasizing the importance of this term. Whether the dwelling is occupied by the owner or rented out, if the loan is secured by such a property, it falls under the purview of TILA, necessitating clear and transparent disclosure of loan terms and costs.

Lastly, a residential mortgage loan is defined as any loan primarily for personal, family, or household use that is secured by a mortgage, deed of trust, or other equivalent consensual security interest on a dwelling or on residential real estate upon which is constructed or intended to be constructed a dwelling. This definition is crucial as it delineates the scope of TILA, focusing on loans that affect consumers' living situations and have significant financial implications.

These terms establish a crucial basis for compliance with TILA. They guarantee that mortgage loan originators and borrowers possess comprehensive knowledge of the complexities associated with mortgage loans, thereby fostering transparency, fairness, and informed decision-making within the real estate finance sector.

Right to Rescind and Seller Contributions

Under the Truth in Lending Act (TILA), the **right to rescind** provides borrowers with a powerful consumer protection mechanism, allowing them to cancel certain credit transactions that involve a lien on their primary residence, with the rescission period typically extending up to three business days following the transaction, the receipt of the rescission notice, or the receipt of all pertinent disclosures, whichever occurs last. This right is pivotal in ensuring borrowers have adequate time to reconsider their commitments and understand the implications of their financial decisions without facing immediate repercussions.

The **rescission notice** must be delivered in a clear and conspicuous manner, outlining the borrower's rights to rescind the transaction, the process for rescission, and the effects of rescission. It should include the deadline by which the borrower must notify the lender of their decision to rescind and highlight that the borrower does not need to provide a reason for rescinding the loan. Lenders are required to provide two copies of the notice of the right to rescind to each party entitled to rescind the transaction.

Refinance rescind scenarios are particularly noteworthy. When a borrower decides to refinance their mortgage with the same lender, the right to rescind applies only to the new credit that exceeds the unpaid principal balance, not to the original loan amount. However, if the refinancing is with a new lender, the entire loan amount is subject to the right of rescission. This distinction underscores the importance of understanding how refinancing impacts borrowers' rescission rights, especially when considering the financial and legal implications of such decisions.

Seller contributions refer to agreements where the seller of a property agrees to pay a portion of the closing costs or offer other financial incentives to the buyer. While not directly related to the right of rescission, understanding seller contributions is crucial for mortgage loan originators and borrowers alike, as these contributions can affect the loan-to-value ratio, the interest rate, and ultimately, the borrower's monthly payments. It's important to note that while seller contributions can facilitate the closing process and make homeownership more accessible, they must be carefully documented and disclosed to ensure compliance with lending regulations and to avoid impacting the borrower's right to rescind.

In practice, the right to rescind is a critical aspect of TILA that ensures borrowers are fully informed and have the opportunity to reconsider their financial decisions. Mortgage loan originators must ensure that borrowers understand their rescission rights and the implications of seller contributions on their loans. Proper documentation and clear communication are essential to navigate these aspects of mortgage transactions, ensuring both compliance with federal laws and the protection of consumers in the mortgage lending process.

HOEPA Protections for High-Cost Mortgages

The Home Ownership and Equity Protection Act (HOEPA), codified under 12 CFR 1026.32, represents a critical segment of consumer protection legislation within the realm of mortgage lending, specifically targeting the regulation of high-cost mortgages. Enacted to address the concerns associated with predatory lending practices, HOEPA sets forth stringent requirements and restrictions for loans that meet certain cost thresholds, thereby safeguarding consumers from potentially exploitative terms.

Under HOEPA, a mortgage is classified as high-cost if its annual percentage rate (APR) or the points and fees charged exceed predefined thresholds. For first-lien mortgages, a loan is considered high-cost if its APR is more than 6.5 percentage points above the average prime offer rate (APOR) for a comparable transaction. For junior liens, the threshold is 8.5 percentage points above the APOR. Additionally, if the total points and fees charged at or before loan closing exceed 5% of the total loan amount for loans of $21,980 or more (this threshold is adjusted annually based on the Consumer Price Index), or the lesser of 8% of the total loan amount or $1,099 for loans below $21,980, the loan is also deemed high-cost under HOEPA.

HOEPA prohibits several practices for high-cost mortgages, aiming to eliminate or reduce predatory lending tactics. Among these prohibitions are the financing of points and fees, which discourages lenders from adding these costs to the loan amount to circumvent upfront payment requirements. The act also bans loan terms that may increase the borrower's risk, such as negative amortization, where the loan principal increases over time, and balloon payments, which require a significantly large payment at the end of the loan term. Additionally, HOEPA restricts the imposition of prepayment penalties, which can financially penalize borrowers for paying off their loans early, and mandates that lenders evaluate a borrower's ability to repay the loan, considering income and expenses beyond the collateral value.

One of the hallmark features of HOEPA is its requirement for enhanced disclosures to borrowers. Lenders must provide a series of disclosures that clearly outline the terms of the high-cost mortgage, including a warning that the loan may have rates and fees higher than other loans, a notice that the lender can take the property if payments are not made, and an advisement to not sign the documents if the terms are not fully understood. These disclosures must be provided at least three business days before the loan is finalized, granting borrowers a critical period to review the terms and seek advice or withdraw from the transaction without penalty.

Moreover, HOEPA facilitates borrower remedies for violations of its provisions, including extended rights of rescission and the ability to recover statutory and actual damages, as well as legal fees in cases of successful litigation against lenders for non-compliance. This enforcement mechanism ensures that lenders adhere to HOEPA's requirements, underpinning the act's role in promoting fair lending practices and protecting consumers from high-cost mortgage terms that could lead to financial distress or the loss of their homes.

In essence, HOEPA's protections for high-cost mortgages are a pivotal component of the regulatory framework governing the lending industry, designed to prevent abusive lending practices and ensure that borrowers are treated fairly. By setting APR and fee thresholds, prohibiting risky loan features, and mandating comprehensive disclosures, HOEPA empowers consumers with the information and protections necessary to make informed decisions about high-cost mortgages, reinforcing the integrity of the mortgage lending process.

Higher-Priced Mortgage Loan Criteria

Higher-priced mortgage loans, as delineated under 12 CFR 1026.35, are subject to specific criteria and rules designed to protect borrowers from potentially onerous lending practices. These loans are characterized by their interest rates, which exceed the Average Prime Offer Rate (APOR) by a certain percentage. Specifically, for first-lien mortgages, a loan qualifies as higher-priced if its annual percentage rate (APR) is 1.5 percentage points or more above the APOR. For second-lien mortgages, the threshold is 3.5 percentage points above the APOR. This distinction is crucial in identifying loans that, due to their higher costs, pose increased risks to borrowers.

The APOR is a benchmark interest rate derived from average interest rates, fees, and other loan terms offered to prime borrowers. It is published weekly by the Federal Financial Institutions Examination Council (FFIEC), providing a standard against which lenders can evaluate the pricing of their mortgage offers. The use of the APOR as a reference point ensures that the determination of whether a loan is considered higher-priced is grounded in current market conditions, thereby offering a dynamic and responsive measure to protect consumers.

For higher-priced mortgage loans, lenders are mandated to establish an escrow account for the payment of property taxes and homeowner's insurance. This requirement is designed to safeguard the interests of both the borrower and the lender by ensuring that funds are available to cover these essential expenses, thereby reducing the risk of tax liens or uninsured losses that could jeopardize the property. The escrow account must be maintained for at least five years, after which it may be waived under certain conditions, such as when the loan-to-value ratio reaches a level deemed safe by the lender.

In addition to escrow requirements, higher-priced mortgage loans are subject to stringent appraisal rules aimed at ensuring the fair valuation of properties. Lenders must obtain a written appraisal from a licensed or certified appraiser who conducts a physical property visit. Furthermore, for properties sold within 180 days of a previous sale at a lower price, lenders are required to obtain an additional appraisal at no cost to the borrower. This second appraisal must provide a detailed analysis of the property's value, including any renovations or improvements made since the prior sale. These appraisal requirements are intended to prevent inflated property valuations that could lead to borrowers being overleveraged and at greater risk of default.

The protections for borrowers under 12 CFR 1026.35 extend beyond escrow and appraisal requirements. Lenders are prohibited from structuring loans with risky features, such as negative amortization or prepayment penalties that exceed specified limits. Additionally, lenders must verify the borrower's ability to repay the loan, considering their income, debts, employment status, and credit history. This verification process is critical in preventing borrowers from being approved for loans that they cannot afford, thereby reducing the incidence of default and foreclosure.

The regulations governing higher-priced mortgage loans represent a concerted effort to balance the need for credit accessibility with the imperative of consumer protection. By setting thresholds based on the APOR, requiring escrow accounts for taxes and insurance, enforcing rigorous appraisal standards, and mandating the verification of borrowers' repayment ability, these rules aim to ensure that higher-priced loans are offered in a manner that is both fair and sustainable. Through these measures, the regulation seeks to protect borrowers from the potential pitfalls of high-cost lending while preserving their access to mortgage credit.

MLO Compensation Rules and Restrictions

Under the regulations set forth in 12 CFR 1026.36(d), part of the Truth in Lending Act (TILA), specific rules govern the compensation of mortgage loan originators (MLOs) to ensure fairness and transparency in the mortgage lending process. These rules are critical for maintaining the integrity of the lending industry and for protecting consumers from unfair practices. The regulation prohibits dual compensation and imposes restrictions on compensation based on loan terms, alongside mandating transparent payment practices.

Dual compensation is prohibited under these regulations, meaning an MLO cannot receive compensation from both the borrower and another party, such as the lender or another third party, in connection with a single mortgage transaction. This rule is designed to prevent conflicts of interest that may arise if an MLO is incentivized to steer borrowers towards specific loan products not because they are in the best interest of the borrower but because they offer the MLO higher compensation.

Furthermore, the regulation restricts MLO compensation based on the terms or conditions of the loan, other than the amount of credit extended. This means that an MLO's compensation cannot be tied to the loan's interest rate, annual percentage rate (APR), or any other loan term. The intent behind this restriction is to discourage MLOs from directing borrowers into higher-cost loans or terms that benefit the MLO at the expense of the borrower. By decoupling MLO compensation from loan terms, the regulation aims to align the MLO's interests more closely with those of the borrower, promoting fairer, more transparent lending practices.

The requirement for transparent payment practices under 12 CFR 1026.36(d) mandates that MLO compensation agreements be clear and disclosed in a manner that is understandable to borrowers. This transparency is crucial for borrowers to make informed decisions about their mortgage loans. It ensures that borrowers are aware of how their MLO is compensated and that this compensation does not influence the loan terms offered to them.

In practice, these regulations necessitate that lenders and MLOs establish compensation agreements that comply with these rules, carefully structuring compensation plans to avoid any prohibited payments or incentives. Lenders must monitor these agreements and the compensation paid to MLOs to ensure ongoing compliance with TILA's requirements. This oversight includes regular audits and reviews of compensation practices to prevent violations that could harm borrowers or lead to regulatory penalties.

The regulations surrounding MLO compensation are a cornerstone of the consumer protection framework within the mortgage lending industry. By prohibiting dual compensation, restricting compensation based on loan terms, and requiring transparent payment practices, 12 CFR

1026.36(d) plays a pivotal role in promoting the fair treatment of borrowers and the integrity of the mortgage process. Compliance with these rules is not only a legal requirement but also a critical component of ethical lending practices that benefit consumers, lenders, and MLOs alike.

TILA-RESPA Integrated Disclosure Rule

Purpose of TRID

The TILA-RESPA Integrated Disclosure Rule, commonly referred to as TRID, represents a significant advancement in the mortgage industry's approach to consumer disclosure. Enacted to integrate the Truth in Lending Act (TILA) and the Real Estate Settlement Procedures Act (RESPA), TRID's primary objective is to streamline the loan disclosure process for consumers, making it more straightforward and easier to understand. This integration aims to enhance borrower comprehension of their loan terms, fees, and other critical information, thereby facilitating a more informed decision-making process.

At the heart of TRID is the consolidation of four previously separate disclosure forms into two main documents: the Loan Estimate and the Closing Disclosure. The Loan Estimate is provided to borrowers within three business days after they submit a loan application. It outlines the estimated interest rates, monthly payments, and closing costs associated with the loan. The aim is to give borrowers a clear, concise overview of the potential costs of their mortgage, enabling them to shop and compare offers from different lenders.

The Closing Disclosure, delivered at least three business days before loan consummation, finalizes the terms and costs of the transaction. This document provides borrowers with the actual terms and costs in a format that is directly comparable to the initial Loan Estimate. This comparison is crucial for borrowers to confirm that the terms have not changed significantly and to ensure they understand the financial commitment they are about to make.

TRID emphasizes transparency and borrower understanding at every stage of the mortgage process. By simplifying the disclosure documents and making them more accessible, TRID aims to prevent the confusion and misunderstanding that can occur with complex loan information. The rule mandates that lenders use clear language and standardized formats to present information, making it easier for borrowers to locate key details such as interest rates, monthly payments, and total closing costs.

Moreover, TRID introduces stricter timing requirements for the delivery of these disclosures. These requirements ensure that borrowers have sufficient time to review their loan details, ask questions, and seek clarification if necessary before proceeding to closing. This period is critical for borrowers to fully grasp the implications of their mortgage agreement and to make informed financial decisions.

The implementation of TRID also serves to protect consumers from unexpected costs at closing. By requiring that the Closing Disclosure be provided three business days before consummation, borrowers are given the opportunity to identify and resolve discrepancies between the estimated and actual costs. This provision helps to eliminate surprises at closing, contributing to a more transparent and predictable lending environment.

In essence, TRID's consolidation and simplification of mortgage disclosures represent a significant step forward in consumer protection and financial literacy. By providing clear, timely, and accurate information about mortgage terms and costs, TRID empowers borrowers to make informed decisions, compare loan offers effectively, and ultimately, to enter into mortgage agreements with a comprehensive understanding of their financial obligations and rights. This alignment of lender transparency with borrower understanding is fundamental to fostering trust in the mortgage process and ensuring the long-term financial well-being of consumers.

Loans Covered Under TRID

The TILA-RESPA Integrated Disclosure Rule (TRID) significantly impacts the majority of closed-end consumer mortgages, establishing a new standard for transparency and borrower understanding throughout the mortgage process. TRID's applicability extends to a wide range of mortgage products, ensuring that borrowers receive consistent and comprehensible information about their loans. However, it is crucial to note the specific exclusions within TRID's scope to fully grasp its impact on the mortgage industry.

Closed-end consumer mortgages, the primary focus of TRID, encompass most traditional home loans where the borrower repays the loan through a series of scheduled payments until the full loan amount is paid off. These include conventional loans, FHA loans, VA loans, and other mortgage products designed for purchasing or refinancing residential properties. Under TRID, lenders originating these loans must provide borrowers with standardized Loan Estimates and Closing Disclosures, facilitating a clearer understanding of loan terms, costs, and risks.

Exclusions from TRID are notably specific, carved out to address particular lending scenarios that do not align with the rule's primary objectives. Among these exclusions are:

- **Home Equity Lines of Credit (HELOCs):** HELOCs operate as open-end credit lines rather than traditional closed-end mortgages, allowing borrowers to draw and repay funds up to a certain limit. Due to their revolving nature and flexible repayment terms, HELOCs are not subject to the same disclosure requirements under TRID.

- **Reverse Mortgages:** Designed for older homeowners to convert part of their home equity into cash without having to sell their home or make monthly mortgage payments, reverse mortgages fall outside TRID's purview. These loans have distinct features and risks, necessitating specialized disclosures not covered by TRID.

- **Loans Made by Small Creditors in Rural or Underserved Areas:** Recognizing the unique challenges and market conditions faced by small lenders in rural or underserved areas, TRID provides exemptions for loans originated by these entities. This exemption aims to prevent undue regulatory burdens that could restrict access to credit in these communities.

Understanding the scope of TRID's applicability and its exclusions is essential for mortgage professionals and borrowers alike. For loans covered under TRID, lenders must adhere to strict timing and content requirements for disclosures, ensuring borrowers have the information needed to make informed decisions. Conversely, recognizing the types of loans exempt from TRID helps industry participants navigate the regulatory landscape more effectively, identifying when alternative disclosure standards apply.

By delineating the boundaries of TRID's applicability, mortgage professionals can better guide borrowers through the lending process, ensuring compliance with regulatory requirements while promoting transparency and borrower understanding. As the mortgage industry continues to evolve, staying informed about such regulatory nuances remains critical for both compliance and consumer protection.

Loan Estimate Breakdown

The Loan Estimate is a critical document designed to provide borrowers with clear and concise information about the expected costs of their mortgage. This document is delivered to the borrower within three business days after they submit a mortgage application, as mandated by the TILA-RESPA Integrated Disclosure Rule (TRID). It serves as a preliminary overview of loan terms, interest rates, monthly payments, and the costs associated with closing the mortgage. The Loan Estimate enables borrowers to compare different offers, fostering an environment of transparency and informed decision-making.

Loan Terms: This section of the Loan Estimate outlines the amount borrowed, the interest rate, and the loan term (e.g., 30 years). It also specifies whether the interest rate is fixed or adjustable, which is crucial for understanding how payments might change over time.

Projected Payments: This part details the payment schedule, including how the monthly payment could change with an adjustable-rate mortgage. It breaks down the principal and interest, mortgage insurance, and estimated escrow to show the total monthly payment. The projection covers the initial period and any changes that might occur if it's an adjustable-rate mortgage.

Costs at Closing: This section provides a summary of the estimated closing costs and the total amount of cash needed at closing. It includes lender fees, points paid to reduce the interest rate, and third-party charges for services like appraisals and title insurance.

Closing Cost Details:
- **Origination Charges**: These are fees charged by the lender for processing the mortgage application. It can include underwriting fees, points to lower the interest rate, and application fees.
- **Services You Cannot Shop For**: Costs for services that the lender chooses, such as the appraisal fee, credit report fee, and flood determination fee.
- **Services You Can Shop For**: Fees for services where the borrower has the option to choose the provider, including title search, pest inspection, and survey fees.
- **Taxes and Government Fees**: This includes recording fees and transfer taxes imposed by state and local governments.
- **Prepaids**: Costs that are paid in advance, such as homeowners insurance premiums and pre-paid interest.
- **Initial Escrow Payment at Closing**: This covers the initial deposit for the escrow account, which will be used to pay ongoing costs like property taxes and homeowners insurance.
- **Other**: Any additional costs, such as homeowners association (HOA) fees, warranty plans, or lender credits.

Calculating Cash to Close: This section provides a detailed calculation of the total amount of money the borrower will need to bring to the closing table. It includes the down payment, closing costs, adjustments for items paid by the seller in advance, and other credits.

Additional Information: The Loan Estimate also contains information about whether the loan has prepayment penalties or balloon payments, which could significantly impact the borrower's financial obligations.

Applicant Information: Essential borrower information, including name, income, social security number (SSN), property address, estimated property value, and loan amount sought, triggers the issuance of the Loan Estimate.

The Loan Estimate is not just a formality; it is a tool for borrowers to use in their decision-making process. By carefully reviewing this document, borrowers can assess the affordability and suitability of the loan offer. It encourages borrowers to ask questions and seek clarification, ensuring they fully understand the terms and obligations of their mortgage before proceeding.

Loan Consummation Definition

Loan consummation marks a pivotal moment in the mortgage process, signifying the point at which the borrower becomes legally bound by the terms of the mortgage agreement. This critical juncture is not merely a formality but a significant legal event, typically occurring at the closing of the loan. The exact timing and definition of loan consummation can vary based on state laws and regulations, underscoring the importance of understanding local legal frameworks.

At its core, loan consummation occurs when the borrower and lender agree to the mortgage terms, and the borrower commits to the loan obligations. This commitment is evidenced by the signing of legal documents, such as the promissory note and mortgage or deed of trust. These documents formalize the borrower's promise to repay the loan under the agreed-upon terms and secure the loan with the property being financed.

State law plays a crucial role in interpreting when loan consummation officially takes place. While the general principle holds that consummation happens at closing, nuances in state regulations may affect the precise moment of legal obligation. For instance, some states may consider loan consummation to occur upon the borrower's signing of the promissory note, while others may pinpoint it at the time of funding or when the borrower takes possession of the loan funds.

Understanding the specific point of loan consummation is essential for both borrowers and lenders, as it triggers several legal rights and responsibilities. For borrowers, it marks the beginning of their obligation to make scheduled loan payments and comply with other terms of the mortgage. For lenders, it signifies the point at which the mortgage becomes enforceable, and they obtain a security interest in the property.

In the context of the TILA-RESPA Integrated Disclosure Rule (TRID), recognizing the moment of loan consummation is critical for ensuring compliance with disclosure timing requirements. Lenders must provide borrowers with the Closing Disclosure at least three business days before loan consummation, allowing borrowers sufficient time to review the final terms of their loan. This requirement emphasizes the significance of accurately determining the consummation date to meet regulatory obligations and protect the borrower's right to informed consent.

CFPB Toolkit Delivery Requirements

The Consumer Financial Protection Bureau (CFPB) mandates the delivery of the "Your Home Loan Toolkit" to borrowers applying for home purchase loans to ensure they are well-informed about the mortgage process. This requirement is integral to the TILA-RESPA Integrated Disclosure Rule, aiming to enhance transparency and borrower understanding in the mortgage industry. The toolkit serves as a comprehensive guide, providing essential information on the nature and costs of real estate transactions, thereby empowering borrowers to make informed decisions.

Upon the submission of a loan application for a home purchase, lenders are obligated to provide applicants with this toolkit within three business days. The timing of this delivery is critical, as it allows borrowers sufficient time to review and comprehend the detailed information before proceeding further in the loan process. The toolkit includes explanations of loan terms, interest rates, monthly payments, and closing costs, alongside guidance on how to shop for different loan offers and compare them effectively.

The "Your Home Loan Toolkit" is not merely a collection of definitions and explanations. It is designed to engage borrowers actively in the mortgage process, encouraging them to ask questions and seek clarification on any aspects they may not understand. This proactive engagement is crucial for navigating the complexities of mortgage transactions and avoiding potential pitfalls.

Moreover, the toolkit addresses the importance of evaluating loan features beyond the interest rate, emphasizing considerations such as loan fees, terms, and the implications of adjustable rates. It also provides practical worksheets and checklists to assist borrowers in organizing their financial information, estimating their affordability, and planning for the future costs associated with homeownership.

By ensuring the delivery of the "Your Home Loan Toolkit," the CFPB underscores its commitment to consumer protection and financial education. This initiative reflects a broader regulatory effort to foster a more transparent, fair, and responsible mortgage market. Lenders must adhere to this requirement not only to comply with federal regulations but also to support their clients' journey toward making one of the most significant financial decisions of their lives.

Closing Disclosure Contents

The Closing Disclosure is a critical document in the mortgage process, designed to provide borrowers with a comprehensive breakdown of the final loan terms, costs, and payment details.

This document is mandated by the TILA-RESPA Integrated Disclosure Rule to ensure transparency and to facilitate borrowers' understanding of their mortgage obligations before finalizing the loan agreement. The Closing Disclosure must align closely with the initial Loan Estimate provided to borrowers, allowing them to compare the estimated and actual costs effectively.

The contents of the Closing Disclosure are meticulously organized into several sections, each serving a specific purpose in outlining the terms of the mortgage. The first section details the borrower and lender information, including names and contact details, alongside the loan term, purpose, product type, and loan type, ensuring all parties are correctly identified and the loan specifics are clearly stated.

Following this, the loan terms section provides a summary of the loan amount, interest rate, and monthly principal and interest payments. This section highlights whether the interest rate is fixed or adjustable and specifies if the loan balance or payment can increase. Any prepayment penalty or balloon payment is also disclosed here, offering a clear understanding of the loan structure.

The projected payments section breaks down the estimated monthly payment over the life of the loan, including principal and interest, mortgage insurance, and any escrow payments for property taxes and homeowner's insurance. This section illustrates how the borrower's payments may change over time, accounting for adjustments in interest rates for adjustable-rate mortgages or changes in escrow account disbursements.

The costs at closing section summarizes the borrower's closing costs, including the total loan costs, other costs like taxes and government fees, and the total amount of cash needed to close. This section is divided further into loan costs, encompassing origination charges, services the borrower did not shop for, and services the borrower did shop for. Other costs cover taxes and government fees, prepaids for homeowner's insurance, property taxes, and initial escrow payment at closing, alongside any other costs like HOA fees or warranties.

A detailed breakdown of the loan calculation is provided, showing the total payments over the loan term, the finance charge, the amount financed, and the annual percentage rate (APR), which represents the cost of the loan as a yearly rate. This calculation helps borrowers understand the total cost of the credit extended to them.

The Closing Disclosure also includes information on whether the lender intends to service the loan or transfer servicing to another lender, alongside disclosures related to appraisal, contract details, liability after foreclosure, and the borrower's right to rescind the loan under certain conditions.

Lastly, the Closing Disclosure contains a section for loan advisor details and an acknowledgment page where the borrower confirms receipt of the document. This acknowledgment does not obligate the borrower to accept the loan but serves as proof that they received the Closing Disclosure outlining the final terms and costs of their mortgage.

The alignment between the Loan Estimate and the Closing Disclosure is crucial, as it ensures borrowers are fully informed of any changes to the loan terms or costs initially provided. This alignment is a key component of the TILA-RESPA Integrated Disclosure Rule, aimed at enhancing borrower understanding and preventing surprises at the closing table. Through the Closing Disclosure, borrowers are equipped with the detailed information necessary to make informed decisions about their mortgage loan.

Disclosures Timing Rules

In compliance with the TILA-RESPA Integrated Disclosure Rule, the timing of disclosures is meticulously regulated to ensure borrowers receive critical information at pivotal moments during the loan application process. This regulation mandates that a Loan Estimate must be delivered to the borrower within three business days following the receipt of a loan application. The definition of a business day in this context encompasses all calendar days except Sundays and legal public holidays. The Loan Estimate serves as a preliminary disclosure, providing the borrower with detailed information about the estimated costs, terms, and risks associated with the mortgage offer. This document is crucial for enabling consumers to compare different loan offers and make informed decisions about proceeding with a mortgage application.

The Closing Disclosure, another critical document in the mortgage process, must be provided to the borrower at least three business days before loan consummation. Loan consummation is the point at which the borrower becomes legally obligated to the loan terms, which may not necessarily coincide with the closing or settlement date. The three-day review period is designed to give borrowers sufficient time to review the final loan terms and costs, ask questions, and ensure they understand their financial commitments before proceeding. This period also allows for the resolution of any discrepancies between the initial Loan Estimate and the final terms presented in the Closing Disclosure.

It is important to note that if there are significant changes to the loan terms after the initial Closing Disclosure has been provided—such as changes to the APR beyond a specified tolerance, the addition of a prepayment penalty, or changes to the loan product itself—a revised Closing Disclosure must be issued, and a new three-business-day review period is triggered. Minor changes, such as corrections to spelling or clerical errors, do not necessitate a new review period.

Lenders must adhere strictly to these timing requirements to remain compliant with federal regulations. Failure to do so can result in regulatory penalties and could potentially delay the closing process. Mortgage professionals and loan originators play a vital role in ensuring that these documents are prepared and delivered in a timely manner, maintaining open communication with the borrower throughout the process.

The precision of these timing rules underscores the regulatory emphasis on transparency and borrower protection within the mortgage lending process. By mandating specific timeframes for the delivery of the Loan Estimate and Closing Disclosure, the TILA-RESPA Integrated Disclosure Rule aims to enhance the borrower's understanding of their mortgage terms and costs, thereby facilitating a more informed and empowered consumer base in the real estate market.

MLO Actions for Incomplete TRID Disclosure

In the event that a TRID disclosure is found to be incomplete or contains errors, it is incumbent upon the mortgage loan originator (MLO) to take immediate and decisive action to rectify these inaccuracies. The TILA-RESPA Integrated Disclosure Rule, a cornerstone of consumer protection in the mortgage process, mandates strict adherence to both the timing and accuracy of disclosures provided to borrowers. This framework is designed to ensure that borrowers are fully informed of the terms and costs associated with their mortgage, thereby facilitating a transparent and fair lending environment.

Upon identification of an incomplete or erroneous disclosure, the MLO must first assess the nature and extent of the discrepancy. This involves a detailed review of the Loan Estimate and Closing Disclosure documents against the actual terms and conditions of the mortgage. Should discrepancies be identified, the MLO is required to prepare and issue revised disclosures. This corrective action must be undertaken promptly to avoid any delays in the mortgage process and to ensure compliance with federal regulations.

The issuance of revised disclosures triggers specific timing requirements that the MLO must adhere to. For instance, if significant changes occur that affect the loan's annual percentage rate (APR), the loan product, or the addition of a prepayment penalty, the borrower must be provided with a new Closing Disclosure reflecting these changes. Importantly, the borrower must receive this revised Closing Disclosure at least three business days before loan consummation. This cooling-off period allows the borrower sufficient time to review the changes and to make an informed decision regarding the mortgage.

Minor changes that do not alter the APR beyond the applicable tolerance threshold, add a prepayment penalty, or change the loan product do not necessitate a new three-business-day waiting period. However, even in these instances, the MLO must ensure that revised disclosures are provided to the borrower at or before closing, thereby upholding the principles of transparency and borrower protection.

In fulfilling their responsibilities under TRID, MLOs must maintain meticulous records of all communications and disclosures made to borrowers. This includes documentation of the reasons for any revisions to disclosures, the specific changes made, and the dates on which revised disclosures were provided to the borrower. Such diligence not only demonstrates compliance with TRID requirements but also serves to protect the MLO and lender in the event of a dispute or regulatory audit.

Moreover, MLOs play a critical role in educating borrowers about the implications of revised disclosures. This involves explaining the nature of the changes, how they affect the borrower's mortgage, and addressing any questions or concerns the borrower may have. By fostering an environment of open communication and transparency, MLOs contribute to a more informed and empowered consumer base, which is central to the objectives of the TILA-RESPA Integrated Disclosure Rule.

In summary, the responsibility of the MLO in the event of incomplete or erroneous TRID disclosures is multifaceted, encompassing the prompt correction of disclosures, adherence to specific timing requirements, meticulous record-keeping, and borrower education. Through diligent compliance with these requirements, MLOs uphold the integrity of the mortgage process, protect consumer interests, and contribute to the overall transparency and fairness of the real estate financing environment.

Change of Circumstances in Loan Estimates

A **change of circumstances** refers to specific events that legally permit or require lenders to revise the Loan Estimate initially provided to the borrower. These events can significantly impact the terms and costs of a mortgage, necessitating an updated disclosure to ensure transparency and compliance with the TILA-RESPA Integrated Disclosure Rule (TRID). Recognized changes of circumstances include, but are not limited to, appraisal changes, borrower decisions, and the discovery of technical errors or omissions in the original Loan Estimate.

Appraisal changes occur when the appraised value of the property significantly differs from the expected value, affecting the loan-to-value ratio (LTV) and potentially the interest rate and loan product eligibility. For instance, if an appraisal comes in lower than anticipated, the LTV ratio may increase, leading to higher interest rates or the need for private mortgage insurance (PMI), which would necessitate a revised Loan Estimate to reflect these new costs.

Borrower decisions that can lead to a change of circumstances include choosing a different loan type than originally applied for, such as switching from a fixed-rate to an adjustable-rate mortgage, or deciding to add a co-borrower to the application. These decisions alter the loan structure and associated costs, requiring an update to the Loan Estimate to accurately represent the new terms.

Upon the occurrence of a valid change of circumstance, lenders are obligated to issue a revised Loan Estimate within three business days. This revision must clearly detail the changes in loan terms and costs resulting from the new circumstances. It's crucial for lenders to document the reason for the change and the specific impact on the Loan Estimate to maintain compliance and transparency.

The revised Loan Estimate must be delivered or placed in the mail to the borrower no later than four business days before loan consummation. If the revised Loan Estimate is not provided to the borrower within the prescribed timeframe, the lender is required to honor the terms and costs as disclosed in the original Loan Estimate, barring any exceptions allowed under TRID.

Lenders must also ensure that the revised Loan Estimate does not include increases in charges that are otherwise prohibited by TRID regulations. For example, charges for third-party services for which the borrower is not allowed to shop and which were selected by the lender cannot increase unless a separate, permissible change of circumstance occurs that directly affects those charges.

The ability to revise a Loan Estimate based on a change of circumstances is a critical component of the mortgage process, ensuring that borrowers receive accurate and up-to-date information regarding their loan terms and costs. Lenders must carefully monitor for any changes that might affect the Loan Estimate and act promptly to update disclosures in accordance with TRID requirements, thus upholding the principles of fairness and transparency in the lending process.

Consumer Rights: Loan Information Requests

Under the TILA-RESPA Integrated Disclosure Rule, borrowers possess specific rights designed to ensure transparency and understanding throughout the loan process. One of these pivotal rights is the ability to request detailed information regarding their loan application, including cost breakdowns and the details of their Loan Estimate. This provision empowers borrowers to actively engage with their mortgage loan originators (MLOs) and lenders, fostering an environment of open communication and informed decision-making.

When a borrower submits a loan application, the lender is obligated to provide a Loan Estimate within three business days. This document is crucial as it outlines the estimated interest rates, monthly payments, and closing costs associated with the loan. However, the borrower's right to information extends beyond the initial receipt of the Loan Estimate. At any point during the loan process, the borrower can request further details or clarification about the costs and terms outlined in the Loan Estimate. This includes, but is not limited to, the breakdown of individual fees, such as origination charges, title insurance fees, and appraisal fees, among others.

Moreover, borrowers have the right to inquire about the status of their loan application. This encompasses updates on the progress of the application, any additional documentation required, and the anticipated timeline for approval. Lenders and MLOs are required to respond to these inquiries promptly, providing accurate and up-to-date information to the borrower.

In addition to the Loan Estimate, borrowers may also request a detailed explanation of any changes that occur during the loan process. For instance, if the terms of the loan or the estimated costs change, leading to a revised Loan Estimate, the borrower has the right to understand the reasons behind these adjustments. This may include changes in interest rates, loan products, or the discovery of information that affects the borrower's creditworthiness.

It is important for borrowers to understand that these rights are not merely procedural formalities but are integral to ensuring that they are fully informed and comfortable with the terms of their mortgage. Lenders and MLOs play a critical role in facilitating this understanding by providing clear, concise, and timely information in response to borrower inquiries.

Furthermore, the TILA-RESPA Integrated Disclosure Rule mandates that lenders and MLOs maintain records of all communications and disclosures related to the loan application. This includes documentation of any information provided to the borrower upon request. Such record-keeping practices are essential for compliance purposes and serve as a safeguard for both the borrower and the lender, ensuring that all parties have access to accurate and consistent information throughout the loan process.

In essence, the borrower's right to request cost breakdowns, Loan Estimate details, and updates on their application status is a fundamental component of the mortgage lending process. It underscores the regulatory emphasis on transparency, borrower protection, and the promotion of an informed consumer base in the real estate market. Lenders and MLOs must be diligent in honoring these rights, providing thorough and accurate information to borrowers upon request, and maintaining open lines of communication to facilitate a smooth and transparent loan process.

Borrower's Right to Rescission

The **right to rescission** grants borrowers the ability to cancel certain types of mortgage transactions within three business days following the closing, the receipt of all required disclosures, or the receipt of the notice of the right to rescind, whichever occurs last. This right is a protective measure under the Truth in Lending Act (TILA), specifically designed to give borrowers a final review period where they can reconsider their commitments without penalty.

For transactions covered under this right, lenders are mandated to provide two copies of the notice of the right to rescission to each party with an ownership interest in the property. The notice must clearly inform borrowers of their right to cancel, how to cancel, and the deadline for cancellation. The rescission period begins only after all parties have received these notices and all relevant material disclosures about the credit contract.

The **three-business-day rescission period** includes Saturdays but excludes Sundays and federal holidays. If the lender fails to provide the required notices or disclosures, the rescission period can be extended up to three years. However, this extended right applies only to the rescission process and does not affect the validity of the loan itself after the rescission period has expired.

Exceptions to the right of rescission include refinancing transactions with the same creditor where no new money is advanced beyond the remaining unpaid principal balance and initial construction loans. Additionally, the right does not apply to the purchase of a new residence or to loans secured by investment properties or second homes.

In the event that a borrower decides to exercise their right to rescission, they must notify the lender in writing within the three-business-day period. Upon receipt of this notice, the lender is required to take steps to terminate the security interest in the property and refund any fees paid by the borrower in connection with the loan transaction. These refunds must be made promptly, typically within 20 calendar days after receipt of the rescission notice.

It is crucial for mortgage loan originators (MLOs) to accurately inform borrowers of their right to rescission and ensure that all disclosures are made in compliance with TILA requirements. Proper execution of these responsibilities not only safeguards the borrower's rights but also upholds the integrity of the lending process. Compliance with the right to rescission is a critical aspect of the mortgage transaction, reflecting the broader commitment to transparency and borrower protection embodied in federal mortgage laws.

Annual Escrow Statement Overview

The annual escrow statement is a critical document for both lenders and borrowers, serving as a comprehensive review of escrow account activity over the past year. This statement is mandated by the TILA-RESPA Integrated Disclosure Rule (TRID) to ensure transparency and compliance with escrow rules. It details the account's beginning balance, itemizes the payments collected for taxes and insurance, and lists disbursements made from the account. Additionally, the statement provides a projection of the upcoming year's payments and any adjustments to the monthly escrow payment amount necessary to cover anticipated disbursements.

One of the primary purposes of the annual escrow statement is to reconcile the account by comparing the projected escrow balance with the actual balance. If there is a surplus, regulations require that amounts over a certain threshold be refunded to the borrower. Conversely, if there is a shortfall, the statement will outline how the deficit will be collected, typically through increased monthly escrow payments.

The statement also plays a vital role in ensuring that borrowers are adequately informed about their escrow account status and the components that influence their overall mortgage payment. By providing a forward-looking estimate of escrow requirements, borrowers can anticipate changes in their monthly mortgage obligations. This foresight is crucial for budgeting and financial planning, particularly for those with fixed incomes or tight budgets.

Compliance with TRID escrow rules through the issuance of the annual escrow statement also helps prevent surprises related to property tax increases or insurance premium adjustments. It ensures that borrowers are not caught off-guard by significant changes in their monthly mortgage payment due to escrow shortages.

In essence, the annual escrow statement facilitates a transparent, informed, and compliant management of escrow accounts, aligning with the overarching goals of TRID to enhance borrower understanding and ensure fair, transparent mortgage lending practices.

Other Federal Laws and Guidelines

Home Mortgage Disclosure Act (HMDA) Overview

The Home Mortgage Disclosure Act (HMDA), codified at 12 CFR Part 1003 (Regulation C), serves a pivotal role in the American financial landscape by mandating the collection, reporting, and public disclosure of loan data by lending institutions. This legislation, initially enacted in

1975, was designed with the primary aim to provide transparency in mortgage lending practices and to ensure that lenders are serving the needs of their communities. HMDA's objectives are multifaceted, focusing on the monitoring of how financial institutions comply with fair lending laws, the facilitation of public investment in local communities, and the aiding of regulatory agencies in enforcing compliance with those laws.

HMDA's purpose extends to the tracking of loan data which encompasses a wide array of information, including but not limited to, the race, ethnicity, and income of loan applicants, the action taken on these loan applications (approved, denied, withdrawn), and the geographic locations of the properties involved. This comprehensive data collection enables regulators and the public to examine and assess how loans and mortgage services are distributed across different demographics and regions, particularly to low and moderate-income neighborhoods. It plays a crucial role in identifying potentially discriminatory lending patterns and ensuring that lenders are not engaging in practices that could be deemed as redlining, wherein lenders avoid providing services to people based on racial or ethnic demographics.

The enforcement of fair lending laws is significantly bolstered by the insights gained from HMDA data. It allows regulatory bodies, such as the Consumer Financial Protection Bureau (CFPB) and the Department of Housing and Urban Development (HUD), to pinpoint discrepancies in lending patterns that may indicate violations of laws like the Equal Credit Opportunity Act (ECOA) and the Fair Housing Act. By analyzing trends and patterns in the data, these agencies can initiate investigations into lenders suspected of discriminatory practices, thereby upholding the principles of fair lending.

Moreover, HMDA data serves as a vital resource for **identifying lending patterns**. It offers a granular view of how mortgage credit is distributed across various sectors of the population, highlighting areas where there may be gaps in service provision. This analysis is instrumental for policymakers and community organizations in understanding the dynamics of the mortgage market and in crafting strategies to address any identified disparities. It also empowers consumers by making loan data accessible, thereby fostering a more competitive and transparent marketplace.

The requirement for lenders to report borrower demographics is a critical aspect of HMDA, as it ensures that there is a clear and accurate representation of who is applying for and receiving loans. This aspect of HMDA underscores the commitment to ensuring that all individuals, regardless of race, ethnicity, or income level, have equitable access to mortgage loans. The demographic data collected also aids in the assessment of whether lenders are meeting the housing needs of the communities they serve, contributing to the broader goal of promoting economic stability and growth.

The Home Mortgage Disclosure Act (HMDA) under Regulation C plays an indispensable role in promoting transparency, fairness, and accountability in the mortgage lending industry. By requiring the systematic reporting of loan data, HMDA helps to enforce fair lending laws, provides valuable insights into lending patterns, and supports the efforts of various stakeholders in making informed decisions aimed at fostering an equitable mortgage market.

Fair Credit Reporting and Consumer Rights

The Fair Credit Reporting Act (FCRA), codified under 15 USC § 1681 et seq., alongside the Fair and Accurate Credit Transactions Act (FACTA), serves as a cornerstone in protecting consumer information and ensuring the accuracy of credit reporting. These statutes are pivotal for mortgage loan originators (MLOs), lenders, and consumers, as they govern the collection, dissemination, and use of credit information across the United States.

Under the FCRA, consumers are afforded a multitude of rights aimed at preserving the integrity of their credit reports. One of the fundamental provisions is the right to access one's credit report. Consumers are entitled to one free report from each of the three major credit reporting agencies (Equifax, Experian, and TransUnion) every 12 months. This access enables individuals to verify the accuracy of the information that could significantly impact their borrowing capabilities.

Accuracy in credit reporting is not merely a consumer privilege but a legal requirement enforced upon credit reporting agencies and data furnishers, which include banks, credit card companies, and other lenders. These entities must take reasonable steps to ensure the information they report is accurate and complete. In instances where inaccuracies are identified, the FCRA mandates a specific dispute resolution process. Consumers can file a dispute with the credit reporting agency, which then has 30 days to investigate the claim and correct any inaccuracies. This process is crucial for rectifying errors that may negatively affect a consumer's credit score and, by extension, their mortgage application outcomes.

Identity theft protection is another critical aspect of the FCRA, further bolstered by FACTA. Consumers have the right to place fraud alerts on their credit reports if they suspect they have been victims of identity theft. This alert notifies potential creditors to take extra steps in verifying the identity of the individual applying for credit. FACTA introduced the right for consumers to place an active duty alert on their credit reports, providing added protection for military personnel who may be at increased risk for identity theft while deployed.

Lenders and MLOs have specific obligations under the FCRA to use reliable credit data when making lending decisions. Before obtaining a consumer's credit report, a lender must have a permissible purpose, such as the evaluation of a credit application. Furthermore, if adverse action is taken based on information contained in a credit report, such as denying a loan application, the lender must provide the consumer with an adverse action notice. This notice must include the name, address, and phone number of the credit reporting agency that supplied the report, a statement that the agency did not make the decision to take the adverse action and cannot provide specific reasons for it, and a notice of the consumer's right to dispute the accuracy or completeness of any information in the report.

For MLOs, understanding and adhering to the FCRA and FACTA requirements is not only a matter of legal compliance but also an ethical obligation to ensure fair and transparent lending practices. Ensuring the accuracy of credit reports, safeguarding against identity theft, and providing clear communication regarding credit decisions are all fundamental to maintaining consumer trust and confidence in the mortgage lending process.

Federal Trade Commission Red Flag Rules

The Federal Trade Commission (FTC) Red Flag Rules, codified at 16 CFR Part 681, mandate that financial institutions and creditors implement a written Identity Theft Prevention Program to identify, detect, and respond to patterns, practices, or specific activities—known as "red flags"—that could indicate identity theft. The primary objective of these rules is to protect consumers and businesses from the damages associated with identity theft, which can range from financial loss to long-term credit impairment.

Under these rules, a "financial institution" is broadly defined to include entities that offer accounts that enable consumers to write checks or make payments to third parties through other means, such as mortgage lending institutions. Similarly, "creditors" encompass businesses or organizations that provide or extend credit to customers. Given the expansive scope of these definitions, a wide array of entities, including mortgage loan originators (MLOs), falls under the purview of the Red Flag Rules.

The Identity Theft Prevention Program must be tailored to the size, complexity, and nature of the financial institution or creditor's operations. The program is required to include reasonable policies and procedures to:

1. **Identify relevant red flags** for new and existing covered accounts and incorporate those red flags into the program. Red flags could include unusual account activity, fraud alerts on a consumer report, or attempts to open an account with suspicious identification.

2. **Detect red flags** that have been incorporated into the program. This involves monitoring the signs of identity theft in the day-to-day operations of the business.

3. **Respond appropriately** to any red flags that are detected to prevent and mitigate identity theft. The response will vary based on the degree of risk posed by the red flag, ranging from monitoring the account more closely to contacting the customer or closing the account.

4. **Ensure the program is updated periodically**, to reflect changes in risks to customers or to the safety and soundness of the creditor or financial institution from identity theft. This includes considering the experiences of the business, changes in the types of accounts offered, and changes in the methods identity thieves employ.

The Red Flag Rules also require that the program be managed by the Board of Directors or senior employees, include staff training, and provide for oversight of service provider arrangements.

For mortgage loan originators, this means incorporating practices such as verifying the identity of applicants, monitoring transactions for signs of identity theft, and ensuring that any third-party service providers they use are also compliant with the Red Flag Rules. It is crucial for MLOs to understand the specific types of red flags that might be encountered in the mortgage process, such as discrepancies in application information, alerts from consumer reporting agencies, or the presentation of suspicious documents.

Compliance with the Red Flag Rules is not just a regulatory requirement but also a critical component of customer service and business integrity. By proactively identifying and responding to potential identity theft, MLOs can protect their clients and their business from the significant harm and inconvenience that identity theft can cause.

BSA/AML: MLO Reporting and Compliance

Under the Bank Secrecy Act (BSA) and Anti-Money Laundering (AML) regulations, Mortgage Loan Originators (MLOs) are required to adopt rigorous practices to prevent financial crimes. These obligations are critical in maintaining the integrity of the financial system and ensuring the trust of the public in mortgage lending practices. MLOs play a pivotal role in identifying and reporting suspicious activities that might indicate money laundering, fraud, or other financial crimes.

Reporting Suspicious Activities: MLOs are mandated to report any transactions that they suspect to be related to money laundering or terrorist financing. This includes transactions that do not have any apparent lawful purpose or are not the sort typically expected for that customer. Suspicious Activity Reports (SARs) must be filed within 30 days of detecting a suspicious transaction. It is crucial for MLOs to document their observations and the reasoning behind the suspicion to comply with SAR filing requirements.

Verifying Customer Identities: One of the cornerstone requirements of BSA/AML compliance is the Customer Identification Program (CIP). MLOs must verify the identity of individuals attempting to conduct financial transactions. This process involves collecting information such as name, date of birth, address, and identification number (e.g., Social Security number for U.S. persons). For non-U.S. persons, other forms of identification might be required, such as a passport number. The verification process should be documented and records retained as prescribed by BSA/AML regulations.

Maintaining Transaction Records: MLOs are required to keep detailed records of transactions for a minimum of five years. This includes documentation related to the customer's identity verification, as well as records of all transactions conducted by the customer. The purpose of maintaining such records is to assist in any future investigations by law enforcement or regulatory bodies into suspicious activities.

Compliance with AML Programs: MLOs are also required to develop, implement, and maintain an effective AML program. This program must be commensurate with the risks posed by the nature and volume of the financial services provided by the MLO. Key components of an AML program include the development of internal policies, procedures, and controls; the designation of a compliance officer; ongoing employee training programs; and an independent audit function to test the program.

The AML program should be tailored to address the specific risks associated with mortgage lending, such as the potential for fraud in loan applications or the use of real estate transactions to launder money. MLOs must conduct regular risk assessments to identify and mitigate the risks of money laundering and terrorist financing specific to their operations.

Continuous Training and Awareness: Ensuring that all staff members are aware of their BSA/AML obligations is critical. Continuous training programs should be in place to keep employees informed about the latest regulatory developments and typologies related to money laundering and financial crimes. Staff should be trained to recognize the signs of suspicious activity and understand the proper channels for reporting such activity.

Compliance with BSA/AML regulations is a critical component of an MLO's operations. By rigorously adhering to these requirements, MLOs not only comply with the law but also contribute to the integrity and stability of the financial system. The responsibilities to report suspicious activities, verify customer identities, maintain transaction records, and implement effective AML programs are fundamental to preventing and detecting financial crimes within the mortgage lending sector.

Gramm-Leach-Bliley Act: Privacy & Compliance

The Gramm-Leach-Bliley Act (GLBA), also known as the Financial Services Modernization Act of 1999, mandates financial institutions to protect the privacy of consumer information and to communicate their information-sharing practices to their customers. The GLBA is pivotal for mortgage loan originators (MLOs) and other entities within the financial services sector, as it directly impacts how consumer information is handled, shared, and protected.

Under the GLBA, financial institutions are required to provide their customers with a privacy notice at the time the customer relationship is established and annually thereafter. This notice must clearly inform customers of the institution's information-sharing practices, including what information is collected, with whom it is shared, and how it is protected. The privacy notice must also explain the methods the institution uses to safeguard personal information. Furthermore, the GLBA grants consumers the right to opt-out of having their personal information shared with non-affiliated third parties, barring certain exceptions.

The safeguarding of consumer data under the GLBA is enforced through the implementation of a comprehensive information security program. This program must be designed to protect the confidentiality, integrity, and availability of consumer information, taking into consideration the size and complexity of the institution's operations. The program should include administrative, technical, and physical safeguards appropriate to the institution's size, complexity, and the nature of its activities. These might include measures such as employee training, secure information processing systems, and physical access controls.

The Federal Trade Commission (FTC) Safeguard Rules further detail the requirements for financial institutions to protect consumer information. These rules require financial institutions to develop, implement, and maintain a written information security plan that describes how the company is prepared for, and plans to continue to protect, customers' personal information. This plan must be relevant to the company's size and complexity, the nature and scope of its activities, and the sensitivity of the customer information it handles.

In addition to privacy and data protection, the GLBA also addresses marketing practices through the Do-Not-Call provisions. These provisions are part of the FTC's Telemarketing Sales Rule (TSR) and provide consumers with the ability to limit telemarketing calls by registering their phone numbers on the National Do Not Call Registry. Financial institutions and MLOs engaging in telemarketing must ensure compliance with the Do-Not-Call provisions, which include honoring the Do Not Call Registry, not calling consumers who have asked not to be called again (company-specific do-not-call requests), and providing caller identification information.

The Do-Not-Call compliance is crucial for MLOs and other financial service providers as it restricts the marketing of personal information in certain telemarketing contexts. Violations of the Do-Not-Call provisions can result in significant penalties, underscoring the importance of adhering to these rules as part of an institution's overall compliance with the GLBA.

The GLBA's comprehensive approach to consumer privacy and protection requires financial institutions, including those in the mortgage lending industry, to be diligent in their handling of personal information. This includes not only safeguarding data but also ensuring transparency with consumers about their privacy practices and respecting consumers' preferences regarding the use and sharing of their information. Compliance with the GLBA is not only a legal requirement but also a critical component of maintaining consumer trust and integrity in the financial services industry.

Mortgage Advertising Regulations

In the realm of mortgage lending and origination, advertising plays a pivotal role in attracting potential borrowers. However, it is governed by stringent regulations to ensure fairness, transparency, and truthfulness in every piece of communication. Under 12 CFR Part 1014, commonly referred to as Regulation N or the Mortgage Acts and Practices – Advertising rule, specific advertising practices are strictly prohibited to protect consumers from misleading, deceptive, or otherwise harmful financial advice and products.

Regulation N delineates clear boundaries for mortgage loan originators (MLOs), lenders, and other entities involved in the mortgage advertising process. One of the core prohibitions under this regulation is the making of false claims or statements. This encompasses any assertions or representations that are factually inaccurate or misleading to the consumer. For instance, an advertisement cannot claim that a mortgage product has a fixed rate when, in fact, it is adjustable or subject to change. Such misrepresentations can lead to consumers making ill-informed decisions, potentially resulting in financial distress or the selection of mortgage products that are not in their best interest.

Material misrepresentations are another critical area addressed by Regulation N. These involve not just outright falsehoods but also omitting important information or presenting data in a way that could mislead or deceive the consumer about the nature, terms, or conditions of a mortgage product. Examples include advertising a low introductory rate without adequately disclosing the conditions under which rates could increase or highlighting the benefits of a loan product without a balanced presentation of the potential risks and downsides.

MLOs bear the responsibility for ensuring that all advertising materials, whether disseminated through traditional media channels, online platforms, or social media, comply with Regulation N. This includes the accurate portrayal of loan terms, the disclosure of all relevant conditions, and the avoidance of any content that could be construed as misleading or deceptive. Moreover, MLOs must be vigilant in their oversight of third-party service providers or affiliates who may be involved in the creation or dissemination of advertising materials on their behalf, as the primary entity is ultimately responsible for compliance with federal advertising standards.

To adhere to these regulations, MLOs and their employing entities should implement comprehensive compliance programs that include regular review and monitoring of advertising materials, training for staff involved in marketing and advertising activities, and swift corrective action when potential violations are identified. Such measures not only ensure adherence to legal requirements but also build trust with consumers by promoting transparency and honesty in mortgage lending practices.

Regulation N serves as a critical safeguard in the mortgage industry, aiming to protect consumers from predatory advertising practices and ensure that they have access to clear, accurate, and useful information when making one of the most significant financial decisions of their lives. By mandating accurate disclosures and prohibiting false claims and material misrepresentations, the regulation upholds the integrity of the mortgage process and fosters a more informed and empowered consumer base.

E-Sign Act: Rules and Legal Equivalence

The Electronic Signatures in Global and National Commerce Act (E-Sign Act) was enacted to facilitate the use of electronic records and signatures in interstate and foreign commerce by ensuring the validity and legal effect of contracts entered electronically. Recognizing the growing reliance on digital transactions, the E-Sign Act establishes that electronic signatures and records are as legally binding as their paper counterparts, provided certain criteria are met. This legislation marks a pivotal advancement in the digitalization of commerce, particularly within the mortgage industry, where the efficiency and security of transactions are paramount.

Under the E-Sign Act, an electronic signature is defined as an electronic sound, symbol, or process, attached to or logically associated with a contract or other record and executed or adopted by a person with the intent to sign the record. This broad definition accommodates various forms of electronic signatures, from typed names at the end of email messages to encrypted digital signatures. For mortgage loan originators (MLOs) and participants in the real estate finance sector, understanding and implementing compliant electronic signature practices is essential for the legality and enforceability of agreements and documents.

Consumer consent plays a critical role in the enforceability of electronic signatures and records. Before obtaining and storing information electronically, businesses must ensure that consumers have affirmatively consented to such practices. The E-Sign Act stipulates that consumers must be provided with clear and conspicuous notice regarding the use of electronic records and must be informed about the hardware and software requirements needed to access and retain electronic records. Only after acknowledging these disclosures and consenting to proceed electronically can the electronic records and signatures be deemed valid.

The legal equivalence of electronic signatures to traditional paper-based signatures under the E-Sign Act removes barriers to electronic commerce, streamlining processes and reducing costs. However, it also imposes responsibilities on businesses to ensure that electronic transactions are conducted in a manner that protects the rights and interests of consumers. For instance, MLOs must ensure that electronic disclosures are delivered in a format that the consumer can access and retain, such as PDF files that can be saved and printed. Additionally, the integrity of the electronic signature process must be maintained, ensuring that signatures are securely linked to their respective records and that any alterations to a document after signing are detectable.

In the context of mortgage lending and origination, the E-Sign Act facilitates a more efficient and accessible process for borrowers and lenders alike. Electronic loan applications, disclosures, and closing documents expedite the lending process, allowing for quicker decision-making and fund disbursement. However, MLOs must be diligent in adhering to the requirements of the E-Sign Act, ensuring that electronic transactions are conducted with transparency, consent, and security to maintain the trust and confidence of consumers in digital mortgage processes.

The adoption of electronic signatures and records, guided by the E-Sign Act, represents a significant shift towards digitalization in the mortgage industry. By understanding and complying with the provisions of the E-Sign Act, MLOs and other industry participants can leverage the benefits of electronic transactions while upholding the legal and ethical standards that protect consumers in the digital age.

USA PATRIOT Act: Identity Verification & Reporting

The USA PATRIOT Act, enacted in response to the September 11, 2001, terrorist attacks, significantly impacts the mortgage industry by setting stringent requirements for customer identity verification, maintaining records, and reporting suspicious financial activities. Under this act, Mortgage Loan Originators (MLOs) and financial institutions are mandated to implement robust programs to prevent, detect, and report potential money laundering and terrorism financing activities. These measures are crucial in maintaining the integrity of the financial system and ensuring compliance with federal regulations.

Customer Identity Verification: The Customer Identification Program (CIP) is a critical component of the USA PATRIOT Act, requiring MLOs to verify the identity of individuals engaging in financial transactions. The verification process involves collecting reliable identification information, such as name, date of birth, address, and identification number (typically a Social Security Number for U.S. persons or a passport number and country of issuance for non-U.S. persons). For mortgage transactions, this means that MLOs must obtain, verify, and record the personal information of their clients at the time of application. The Act stipulates that documents used for verification must be from independent sources, and MLOs should have reasonable belief that the identity of the customer is true and accurate.

Maintaining Records: The act requires that records of the identity verification process be maintained for five years after the account is closed. This includes copies of any document used in verifying the customer's identity, a description of any non-documentary methods used to verify identity, and a record of the resolution of any substantive discrepancies discovered during the verification process. These records are essential for law enforcement and regulatory agencies in investigations and audits to ensure compliance with anti-money laundering (AML) regulations and the prevention of terrorism financing.

Reporting Suspicious Financial Activity: The USA PATRIOT Act enhances the requirements for reporting suspicious activities that may involve money laundering or terrorism financing. Financial institutions, including those involved in mortgage lending, are required to file Suspicious Activity Reports (SARs) with the Financial Crimes Enforcement Network (FinCEN) upon detecting transactions that may involve funds derived from illegal activities or are intended to hide funds derived from illegal activities. Indicators of suspicious activity can include transactions that do not make economic sense, have no apparent lawful purpose, or involve the use of the financial institution to facilitate criminal activity. MLOs play a crucial role in detecting and reporting suspicious activities, as they are often the first point of contact with the customer.

In practice, MLOs should be trained to recognize the signs of money laundering and terrorism financing and understand their responsibilities under the USA PATRIOT Act. This includes conducting due diligence on customers, monitoring transactions for suspicious activities, and knowing when and how to file SARs. Compliance programs should be tailored to the size and risk profile of the institution, with regular audits to ensure that procedures are followed correctly.

The implementation of the USA PATRIOT Act's provisions within the mortgage industry underscores the critical role financial institutions play in national security efforts. By adhering to these requirements, MLOs and their employers not only comply with federal law but also contribute to the broader fight against terrorism financing and money laundering activities.

Homeowners' Protection Act: PMI Cancellation

The Homeowners' Protection Act, commonly referred to as the PMI Cancellation Act, was established to provide homeowners with the right to request the cancellation of Private Mortgage Insurance (PMI) once they have attained a certain level of equity in their home. This act is pivotal for borrowers as it outlines a clear path to reducing their monthly mortgage expenses by eliminating the PMI payments that do not contribute to the principal balance of the mortgage or to the equity of the home.

Under the provisions of the Homeowners' Protection Act, borrowers have the right to request the cancellation of their PMI when the principal balance of their mortgage reaches 80% of the original value of their home, which is typically equated to having 20% equity. This request is subject to certain conditions set forth by the lender, including a good payment history and the absence of any second mortgages or liens against the property. It's imperative for borrowers to understand that the request for PMI cancellation must be made in writing, and the lender may require an appraisal at the borrower's expense to confirm that the home's value has not declined below its original value.

Furthermore, the act mandates automatic termination of PMI when the principal balance of the mortgage is scheduled to reach 78% of the original value of the home, irrespective of the current market value. This automatic termination is a safeguard for borrowers, ensuring that PMI payments are not extended beyond the point where they have accumulated 22% equity under the original amortization schedule of the loan. It is important to note that this automatic cancellation does not require any action from the borrower, such as a request or an appraisal, making it a critical component of the act that provides a fail-safe for homeowners to cease PMI payments when they are legally entitled to do so.

The Homeowners' Protection Act also stipulates that lenders must provide borrowers with an annual written statement that informs them of their rights under the act, including how to initiate a request for PMI cancellation. This annual disclosure is designed to keep borrowers informed about their progress towards reaching the equity thresholds required for PMI cancellation and automatic termination.

For borrowers who are looking to expedite the cancellation of PMI, additional payments towards the principal balance of the mortgage can be made to reach the 20% equity threshold sooner. However, it is essential for borrowers to communicate with their lender regarding any additional payments to ensure that they are applied correctly to the principal balance and to verify how these payments affect the timeline for PMI cancellation eligibility.

The Homeowners' Protection Act empowers borrowers by providing a legal framework for the cancellation and automatic termination of PMI, offering a pathway to reduce monthly mortgage expenses. Borrowers should proactively manage their mortgage payments and communicate with their lenders to take full advantage of the rights and protections afforded by the act.

Dodd-Frank Act: CFPB and Lending Standards

The Dodd-Frank Wall Street Reform and Consumer Protection Act, commonly referred to as the Dodd-Frank Act, was enacted in 2010 in response to the financial crisis of 2008. A cornerstone of this comprehensive legislation is the creation of the Consumer Financial Protection Bureau (CFPB), an agency charged with overseeing financial markets for consumer products, including mortgages. The CFPB's mandate includes enforcing consumer protection laws and ensuring that consumers are treated fairly in the financial marketplace.

One of the critical areas addressed by the Dodd-Frank Act is the prohibition of unfair lending practices that were partly responsible for the mortgage crisis. These practices included making loans without verifying a borrower's ability to repay, steering borrowers towards more expensive loans, and engaging in discriminatory lending practices. The Act introduced several measures to combat these practices and protect consumers.

Ability-to-Repay (ATR) Rule: Central to the Dodd-Frank Act's provisions is the Ability-to-Repay rule. This rule requires lenders to make a reasonable and good faith determination, based on verified and documented information, that the borrower has the ability to repay the loan. Lenders must consider eight specific underwriting factors when making this determination, including the borrower's income or assets, employment status, monthly mortgage payment, monthly payments on simultaneous loans, monthly payments for mortgage-related obligations, current debt obligations, debt-to-income ratio, and credit history.

Qualified Mortgage (QM) Standards: The Act also established Qualified Mortgage (QM) standards, designed to provide safer and more sustainable home loans by prohibiting or limiting certain high-risk products and features. For example, QM loans cannot have terms that exceed 30 years, must not have negative amortization or interest-only features, and generally must limit upfront points and fees to no more than 3% of the total loan amount. Additionally, for a loan to be considered a QM, a borrower's debt-to-income ratio cannot exceed 43%. QM loans are presumed to comply with the ATR requirements, providing lenders with certain legal protections against claims from borrowers who allege that the lender failed to assess their ability to repay the loan.

The Dodd-Frank Act and the CFPB's implementation of its provisions represent a significant shift in the regulatory landscape for mortgage lending. These changes aim to prevent the types of abusive lending practices that contributed to the housing crisis, promote stability in the housing market, and protect consumers from unfair, deceptive, or predatory lending practices. Mortgage Loan Originators (MLOs) must be thoroughly familiar with these regulations, as compliance is not only a legal requirement but also a critical component of ethical lending practices that contribute to the long-term success of the mortgage industry.

Regulatory Authority

CFPB's Role in Mortgage Law Enforcement

The Consumer Financial Protection Bureau (CFPB) plays a pivotal role in the enforcement of federal mortgage laws, oversight of Mortgage Loan Originator (MLO) practices, and the promotion of transparency and borrower protection within the mortgage industry. Established under the Dodd-Frank Wall Street Reform and Consumer Protection Act of 2010, the CFPB's mandate encompasses a wide range of activities designed to ensure that consumers are treated fairly in the financial marketplace and that they have access to clear, accurate, and actionable information when making decisions about mortgage loans.

One of the primary responsibilities of the CFPB is to enforce federal mortgage laws such as the Truth in Lending Act (TILA), the Real Estate Settlement Procedures Act (RESPA), and the Equal Credit Opportunity Act (ECOA), among others. These laws are designed to protect consumers from unfair, deceptive, or abusive practices (UDAAPs) and to ensure that they are provided with timely and understandable information regarding the cost and terms of mortgage loans. The CFPB's enforcement activities include investigating complaints, conducting examinations of mortgage lenders and servicers, and taking enforcement actions against entities that violate the law.

In addition to enforcement, the CFPB oversees MLO practices to ensure compliance with federal standards. This includes monitoring how MLOs are compensated, ensuring that they are not steering consumers into inappropriate mortgage products, and verifying that MLOs are properly licensed and meet the educational and ethical standards set forth in the Secure and Fair

Enforcement for Mortgage Licensing Act (SAFE Act). The CFPB also provides guidance and regulations to help MLOs understand their responsibilities under the law.

Transparency is another key area of focus for the CFPB. The bureau has implemented several initiatives to make the mortgage process more understandable for consumers. This includes the "Know Before You Owe" project, which simplified and combined the disclosures that consumers receive when applying for and closing on a mortgage. The Loan Estimate and Closing Disclosure forms, which are part of this project, provide clear and concise information about the costs and risks of mortgage loans, helping consumers to compare offers and make informed decisions.

The CFPB also plays a critical role in regulating disclosures related to mortgage loans. This includes ensuring that lenders provide accurate and timely information about interest rates, fees, and other loan terms, as well as disclosures related to the transfer of loan servicing and the right to rescind certain mortgage transactions. The CFPB's regulations and guidance help to standardize the information that consumers receive, promoting fairness and transparency in the mortgage market.

Moreover, the CFPB is tasked with protecting borrowers throughout the life of their mortgage. This includes overseeing the practices of mortgage servicers to ensure that they are providing accurate statements, processing payments correctly, and handling loss mitigation applications in accordance with federal guidelines. The CFPB also addresses issues related to mortgage servicing transfers, escrow accounts, and foreclosure prevention efforts.

The CFPB's comprehensive approach to overseeing the mortgage industry reflects its commitment to ensuring that consumers are protected from unfair practices, provided with clear and accurate information, and treated fairly in their interactions with mortgage lenders and servicers. Through its enforcement actions, regulatory guidance, and consumer education efforts, the CFPB aims to promote a more transparent, fair, and responsive mortgage market for all participants.

HUD: Fair Housing and FHA Loan Regulation

The Department of Housing and Urban Development (HUD) plays a pivotal role in the landscape of the U.S. housing market, particularly in the realms of fair housing enforcement, regulation of Federal Housing Administration (FHA) loans, promoting equal access to housing, and providing comprehensive guidance on compliance with the Real Estate Settlement Procedures Act (RESPA). HUD's mission, deeply embedded in its legislative and regulatory frameworks, is to create strong, sustainable, inclusive communities and quality affordable homes for all. This mission directly impacts mortgage loan originators (MLOs) and their practices, necessitating a thorough understanding of HUD's functions and regulations to ensure compliance and promote ethical lending practices.

Fair housing enforcement is a cornerstone of HUD's efforts to eliminate housing discrimination and promote economic opportunity. Under the Fair Housing Act, HUD investigates complaints against housing providers, including lenders, who are accused of engaging in discriminatory practices based on race, color, national origin, religion, sex, familial status, or disability. For MLOs, this underscores the importance of equitable lending practices and the necessity of adhering to strict non-discrimination policies. MLOs must ensure that loan products are offered to qualified applicants on equal terms, without bias or prejudice, to avoid severe penalties and reputational damage.

In regulating FHA loans, HUD oversees one of the most significant programs enabling Americans to access homeownership. FHA loans are government-backed mortgages that offer lower down payments and are more accessible to borrowers with less-than-perfect credit scores. MLOs working with FHA loans must navigate a set of specific requirements, including minimum credit scores, down payment percentages, and mortgage insurance premiums, all designed to protect the lender and the borrower. Understanding the nuances of FHA loan requirements is crucial for MLOs to effectively guide their clients through the loan application process and ensure compliance with HUD's standards.

Promoting equal access to housing is another critical area of HUD's work, closely tied to its fair housing enforcement efforts. This involves not only combating discrimination but also addressing issues of housing affordability and availability. MLOs play a role in this by making mortgage products accessible to a broader spectrum of the population, including underserved communities. By offering a range of loan products and working to understand the unique needs of diverse populations, MLOs can contribute to HUD's goal of equal access to housing.

Guidance on RESPA compliance is perhaps one of the most direct interactions MLOs have with HUD. RESPA, enforced by HUD, requires that consumers receive disclosures at various times in the transaction process and prohibits certain practices that could increase the cost of mortgage settlement services. MLOs must be familiar with RESPA requirements, including those related to good faith estimates, settlement statements, and prohibitions against kickbacks and unearned fees. Compliance with RESPA not only ensures legal and regulatory adherence but also promotes transparency and fairness in the mortgage process, aligning with HUD's broader objectives.

HUD's multifaceted role in fair housing enforcement, FHA loan regulation, promoting equal housing access, and providing guidance on RESPA compliance has a significant impact on the daily operations and ethical responsibilities of mortgage loan originators. Adhering to HUD's regulations and supporting its mission to create inclusive communities and affordable homes allows MLOs to play a vital part in fostering a more equitable and accessible housing market.

Chapter 2: Uniform State Content

SAFE Act

SAFE Act: Purpose and Scope

The Secure and Fair Enforcement for Mortgage Licensing Act, commonly known as the SAFE Act, was enacted on July 30, 2008, as part of the Housing and Economic Recovery Act (HERA) to address the nationwide crisis in the mortgage industry. The primary objective of the SAFE Act is to enhance consumer protection and reduce fraud by establishing minimum standards for the licensing and registration of state-licensed mortgage loan originators (MLOs). It mandates the creation of a Nationwide Multistate Licensing System and Registry (NMLS) to facilitate the licensing process, promote uniformity across states, ensure comprehensive supervision of MLOs, and provide a centralized system for consumers to verify the credentials of mortgage professionals.

The SAFE Act requires all MLOs to register with the NMLS, obtain a unique identifier, and maintain this registration annually. This process includes submitting fingerprints for a criminal background check, completing pre-licensing education courses, passing a comprehensive examination, and demonstrating financial responsibility. The Act aims to ensure that individuals who have a history of fraud or who have engaged in unethical lending practices are prohibited from working in the mortgage industry. By setting these national standards, the SAFE Act seeks to foster trust and confidence among consumers, knowing that they are dealing with qualified and vetted professionals.

Furthermore, the SAFE Act's provisions extend to the transparency and accountability of mortgage loan originators. It requires MLOs to disclose their unique identifier to consumers, which allows the public to access information about their licensing status, disciplinary actions, and employment history through the NMLS Consumer Access portal. This level of transparency is pivotal in empowering consumers to make informed decisions when choosing a mortgage professional to work with.

In addition to enhancing consumer protection, the SAFE Act promotes uniformity and streamlines the licensing process across different states. Before the enactment of the SAFE Act, the requirements for becoming a licensed MLO varied significantly from one state to another, creating confusion and making it difficult for MLOs to operate in multiple states. By establishing a uniform set of national standards, the SAFE Act simplifies the process for MLOs to obtain and maintain licensure in multiple states, thereby encouraging a more efficient and competitive mortgage industry.

The SAFE Act also addresses the need for continuous professional development among mortgage loan originators. It mandates that MLOs complete continuing education courses annually to maintain their license. This requirement ensures that MLOs stay current with the latest developments, laws, and ethical standards in the mortgage industry, further safeguarding consumers and upholding the integrity of the mortgage lending process.

Through the implementation of the SAFE Act and the establishment of the NMLS, the mortgage industry has witnessed significant improvements in the oversight of MLOs, the protection of consumers, and the standardization of licensing requirements. The Act represents a critical step forward in restoring confidence in the mortgage market, enhancing the professionalism of the industry, and ensuring that consumers receive fair and ethical treatment in their mortgage transactions.

Public Record Filing Requirements

The Secure and Fair Enforcement for Mortgage Licensing Act (SAFE Act) necessitates a high level of transparency and accountability from mortgage loan originators (MLOs) to protect consumers and ensure the integrity of the mortgage industry. This transparency is achieved, in part, through the requirement for MLOs to file specific documents for public record. These documents include MLO license applications, financial statements, criminal background checks, and employment history. The filing of these documents for public record serves multiple purposes, including enhancing consumer protection, promoting industry integrity, and facilitating regulatory oversight.

MLO license applications are a cornerstone of this documentation, providing detailed information about the applicant, including personal identification, professional history, and any past regulatory actions or criminal offenses. The application process is designed to vet candidates thoroughly, ensuring that only those who meet the stringent criteria set forth by the SAFE Act are granted the privilege to operate within the mortgage industry. The public availability of these applications allows consumers to verify the credentials of their chosen MLOs, fostering a sense of trust and security in their professional relationships.

Financial statements filed by MLOs offer a snapshot of their financial health and stability. These documents are crucial for regulators to assess the risk profile of individual MLOs, ensuring that they are financially sound and capable of conducting business in a manner that protects consumers from potential fraud or bankruptcy. The public disclosure of financial statements also serves to deter financial irresponsibility among MLOs, as their financial dealings are subject to scrutiny by both regulators and the public.

Criminal background checks are another critical component of the documentation required for public record. These checks help to filter out individuals with histories of financial crime, fraud, or other criminal activities that could pose a risk to consumers. By mandating that these background checks are made public, the SAFE Act ensures that consumers have the ability to make informed decisions about whom they are entrusting with their financial information and mortgage planning.

Employment history filings provide a comprehensive view of an MLO's professional background, including previous positions held within the industry, duration of employment, and reasons for leaving. This information is invaluable for assessing an MLO's experience, reliability, and professional conduct. Public access to employment history helps consumers and regulators alike to identify patterns of behavior that might indicate potential issues, such as frequent job changes without reasonable cause or termination due to misconduct.

The requirement for these documents to be filed for public record under the SAFE Act is a testament to the commitment of the mortgage industry to uphold the highest standards of transparency, integrity, and consumer protection. By making such information readily accessible, the Act empowers consumers, fosters a culture of accountability among MLOs, and aids regulatory bodies in their oversight functions. This framework not only protects consumers but also enhances the reputation of the mortgage industry as a whole, promoting trust and confidence among all stakeholders.

State Mortgage Regulatory Agencies

Regulatory Powers and Responsibilities

State agencies play a pivotal role in the oversight and regulation of Mortgage Loan Originators (MLOs) within the mortgage industry, a sector that is critical to the financial stability and homeownership dreams of many Americans. These regulatory bodies are vested with significant powers and responsibilities to ensure that MLOs adhere to both state and federal laws, thereby safeguarding the interests of consumers and maintaining the integrity of the mortgage lending process.

The licensing of MLOs is a primary function of state mortgage regulatory agencies. This process involves a thorough evaluation of an applicant's background, including criminal history checks, credit assessments, and the verification of educational qualifications. The aim is to ensure that only individuals who meet a high standard of professionalism and ethical conduct are permitted to operate within the industry. State agencies require MLOs to pass a comprehensive exam that covers a wide range of topics relevant to mortgage lending, including federal laws, mortgage products, ethical practices, and the understanding of complex financial concepts. This rigorous screening process is designed to protect consumers from fraud and malpractice and to instill confidence in the mortgage lending system.

Enforcing compliance with laws and regulations is another critical responsibility of state mortgage regulatory agencies. These entities monitor the activities of licensed MLOs to ensure adherence to lending standards and consumer protection laws. Compliance is enforced through regular audits, reviews of lending practices, and the scrutiny of loan documentation. State agencies have the authority to impose sanctions, fines, or even revoke licenses in cases where MLOs are found to be in violation of regulatory requirements. This enforcement mechanism serves as a deterrent against unethical behavior and promotes a culture of accountability and transparency within the industry.

Conducting investigations into alleged misconduct or complaints against MLOs constitutes a significant aspect of the regulatory powers of state agencies. These investigations are initiated based on consumer complaints, reports from other industry participants, or as a result of findings from compliance audits. State agencies have the authority to subpoena documents, interview witnesses, and gather evidence as part of their investigative processes. The outcome of these investigations can lead to disciplinary actions against MLOs, including fines, suspension, or revocation of licenses. Through these investigations, state agencies work to resolve disputes, address consumer grievances, and take corrective action to prevent future occurrences of misconduct.

Protecting consumers in mortgage transactions is the overarching goal of state mortgage regulatory agencies. These bodies implement a range of measures designed to ensure that consumers are treated fairly, receive accurate and transparent information about mortgage products, and are not subjected to deceptive or predatory lending practices. State agencies provide educational resources to consumers, offer guidance on navigating the mortgage process, and maintain public records of licensed MLOs and any disciplinary actions taken against them. By regulating MLOs and enforcing compliance with laws, state agencies play a crucial role in preventing financial exploitation and in promoting the welfare of consumers in the mortgage market.

In fulfilling their regulatory powers and responsibilities, state mortgage regulatory agencies operate within a framework that balances the need for oversight with the promotion of a healthy, competitive mortgage industry. Their efforts to license, monitor, investigate, and enforce compliance among MLOs are essential for maintaining the integrity of the mortgage lending process, protecting consumers, and ensuring the stability of the housing market.

NMLS Registry and State Regulators

The Nationwide Multistate Licensing System & Registry (NMLS) serves as the cornerstone of the regulatory framework for mortgage loan originators (MLOs) across the United States. Established to enhance consumer protection, promote efficiency, and streamline the licensing process, the NMLS functions as a comprehensive central licensing system that facilitates the coordination between state regulatory agencies and the mortgage industry. Its role in tracking MLO activity and ensuring compliance with both federal and state regulations is pivotal in maintaining the integrity of the mortgage lending process.

At the heart of the NMLS's functionality is its ability to provide a standardized, secure platform for the management of licensing information and compliance documentation for individuals and companies engaged in the mortgage industry. This system allows for the collection, monitoring, and sharing of regulatory information among state agencies, thereby promoting uniformity and transparency in the licensing process. Through the NMLS, state regulators can access up-to-date information on MLOs, including their licensing status, disciplinary actions, and employment history. This centralized database is instrumental in aiding state agencies in their oversight responsibilities, ensuring that MLOs meet the stringent requirements set forth by both the Secure and Fair Enforcement for Mortgage Licensing Act (SAFE Act) and state-specific regulations.

The collaboration between the NMLS and state regulatory agencies is characterized by a dynamic partnership that supports the dual goals of consumer protection and industry oversight. State agencies rely on the NMLS for comprehensive data that aids in the evaluation of license applications, the monitoring of compliance with continuing education requirements, and the enforcement of legal and regulatory standards. In turn, the NMLS is continually updated with information from state agencies, ensuring that its records accurately reflect the current status of MLOs nationwide. This reciprocal flow of information enhances the ability of state regulators to conduct thorough investigations, perform audits, and take disciplinary actions when necessary.

Furthermore, the NMLS plays a critical role in facilitating compliance with the SAFE Act's mandate for MLOs to obtain and maintain a unique identifier. This identifier, which remains with an MLO throughout their career, enables consumers to easily access public information regarding mortgage professionals, thereby fostering transparency and accountability. The NMLS Consumer Access portal, a publicly accessible database, allows individuals to verify the credentials of MLOs, enhancing consumer confidence and trust in the mortgage lending process.

In addition to its regulatory and oversight functions, the NMLS serves as an educational resource for both MLOs and state agencies. It offers training and support to ensure that users are proficient in navigating the system and understanding its features. This educational component is essential for maintaining high standards of professionalism within the mortgage industry and ensuring that MLOs are well-informed about regulatory requirements and best practices.

The NMLS's impact extends beyond regulatory compliance and consumer protection. By standardizing the licensing process and fostering a cooperative environment between state agencies and the mortgage industry, the NMLS contributes to a more efficient, accessible, and competitive mortgage market. Its role in tracking MLO activity and compliance is a testament to the commitment of regulatory authorities to uphold the highest standards of integrity and professionalism in the mortgage lending sector. Through its comprehensive database and collaborative framework, the NMLS ensures that state regulators are equipped with the tools necessary to oversee a dynamic and evolving industry, ultimately benefiting consumers and stakeholders alike.

Frequency of Exams

State regulators possess the authority to conduct annual or periodic examinations of Mortgage Loan Originators (MLOs) and their affiliated companies to ensure adherence to both state and federal laws governing the mortgage industry. This regulatory oversight is a critical component of the licensing framework designed to uphold the integrity, competence, and professionalism within the mortgage sector.

The frequency and scope of these examinations are determined by several factors, including the regulatory agency's policies, the MLO's or company's compliance history, and any emerging trends or concerns within the mortgage market that may warrant closer scrutiny. Typically, these exams aim to verify that MLOs and their companies are operating in compliance with laws such as the Truth in Lending Act (TILA), Real Estate Settlement Procedures Act (RESPA), and the Secure and Fair Enforcement for Mortgage Licensing Act (SAFE Act), among others.

During an examination, state regulators may review a wide range of documentation and processes. This can include, but is not limited to, loan files, to ensure proper disclosures were made to consumers; advertising materials, to confirm compliance with marketing regulations; and employee records, to verify that all individuals involved in mortgage origination are properly licensed and have undergone the necessary background checks.

Furthermore, these examinations assess the adequacy of the company's internal policies and procedures related to consumer protection, such as data privacy measures, complaint handling processes, and the implementation of anti-money laundering programs as required under the Bank Secrecy Act (BSA)/Anti-Money Laundering (AML) regulations.

Should a state regulator identify non-compliance or areas of concern during an examination, they have the authority to take corrective actions. These actions can range from issuing a notice of deficiency and requiring the MLO or company to address the issues within a specified timeframe, to imposing penalties, suspending or revoking licenses, and, in severe cases, referring matters for criminal prosecution.

It is incumbent upon MLOs and their companies to maintain a posture of continuous compliance and to engage proactively with regulatory bodies. This includes staying abreast of changes in legislation and regulatory guidance, regularly reviewing and updating internal policies and procedures, and ensuring that all staff are adequately trained on compliance matters.

State regulators' authority to conduct these exams underscores the collaborative effort between regulatory bodies and industry participants to protect consumers and maintain the integrity of the mortgage lending process. Compliance with state and federal laws not only mitigates the risk of regulatory action but also enhances the reputation of MLOs and their companies, fostering consumer trust and confidence in the mortgage industry.

MLO Unique Identifiers and Their Purpose

Mortgage Loan Originators (MLOs) are assigned unique identifiers through the Nationwide Multistate Licensing System & Registry (NMLS) as a foundational aspect of the regulatory framework established under the Secure and Fair Enforcement for Mortgage Licensing Act (SAFE Act). These unique identifiers serve multiple critical functions in the oversight and regulation of the mortgage industry, enhancing both transparency and accountability.

The primary purpose of these unique NMLS identifiers is to facilitate the tracking of MLO activities across different states and regulatory jurisdictions. This tracking capability is essential for regulatory authorities to monitor compliance with both federal and state mortgage lending laws and regulations. By assigning a permanent, unchanging identifier to each MLO, the NMLS ensures that an MLO's record of compliance, including any disciplinary actions or sanctions, is accessible regardless of any changes in employment or state of licensure.

Furthermore, the use of unique identifiers promotes transparency within the mortgage industry. Consumers can use these identifiers to access information about their MLO, including their licensing status and any regulatory actions taken against them. This transparency empowers consumers to make informed decisions when choosing an MLO to work with, fostering trust in the mortgage process.

The unique identifiers also facilitate the linking of MLOs to their licensing and enforcement records within the NMLS database. This linkage is crucial for state and federal regulators in their oversight functions, allowing for efficient and effective supervision of MLOs. Regulators can quickly access an MLO's history, streamline the licensing process, and coordinate enforcement actions when necessary. This system of linked records supports a cohesive regulatory environment that can adapt to the dynamic nature of the mortgage industry.

In addition to regulatory and consumer benefits, the unique NMLS identifiers aid in the prevention of fraud within the mortgage industry. By ensuring that each MLO is uniquely identifiable, the system makes it more difficult for individuals to evade accountability by moving between states or changing employers. This deterrent against fraudulent activity is a key component of the overall strategy to maintain the integrity of the mortgage lending process.

The implementation of unique NMLS identifiers represents a significant advancement in the regulatory infrastructure governing the mortgage industry. By providing a tool for tracking, transparency, and accountability, these identifiers play a pivotal role in upholding the standards of professionalism and integrity that are essential for the protection of consumers and the health of the mortgage market.

CFPB Loan Originator Rule: Dual Compensation

The Consumer Financial Protection Bureau (CFPB) plays a pivotal role in regulating the activities of Mortgage Loan Originators (MLOs) through the enforcement of the Loan Originator Rule, particularly focusing on the prohibition of dual compensation and setting limits on bonuses tied to loan terms. This regulatory framework is designed to ensure that MLOs engage in fair compensation practices, thereby protecting consumers from potential conflicts of interest that could arise from MLO compensation structures.

Dual compensation, in the context of the mortgage industry, refers to the practice where an MLO receives compensation from both the borrower and another party, such as the lender, in a single mortgage transaction. The CFPB's Loan Originator Rule strictly prohibits this practice to prevent any incentive for MLOs to steer borrowers into mortgage loans that are not in their best interest but may offer higher compensation to the MLO. This rule is grounded in the principle that MLOs' compensation should not vary based on the terms or conditions of the loan other than the amount of credit extended. The rule aims to eliminate any potential for MLOs to be influenced by compensation structures that could lead them to prioritize their financial gain over the borrower's needs.

Furthermore, the CFPB sets clear limits on bonuses and other incentive-based compensation that can be tied to the terms of the mortgage loans MLOs originate. The regulation specifies that compensation cannot be based on the interest rate or other loan terms. This is to ensure that the advice and products offered by MLOs to consumers are based on the consumers' best interests rather than the potential for increased compensation for the MLO. However, the rule does allow for certain exceptions, such as contributions to a qualified plan, which are not deemed to be based on the terms of multiple transactions by a single originator.

The enforcement of fair compensation practices under the CFPB's oversight involves rigorous monitoring and auditing of MLO compensation agreements and practices. The CFPB has the authority to conduct examinations of lenders and MLOs to ensure compliance with the Loan Originator Rule. In cases where violations are found, the CFPB can take enforcement actions that may include fines, penalties, and directives to change compensation practices to align with regulatory requirements.

The CFPB's oversight extends to ensuring transparency in how MLOs are compensated. Lenders are required to maintain records of compensation agreements with MLOs for a minimum of three years. This record-keeping requirement supports the CFPB's efforts to monitor and enforce compliance with the dual compensation prohibition and compensation limits. It also provides a mechanism for auditing and accountability, enabling the CFPB to trace and scrutinize the compensation structures and practices within the mortgage industry.

The CFPB's authority under the Loan Originator Rule concerning dual compensation and the restrictions on bonuses related to loan terms represents a vital aspect of the regulatory framework for the mortgage industry. This authority emphasizes the importance of aligning MLO compensation practices with the best interests of consumers, thereby fostering transparency, fairness, and integrity in the mortgage loan origination process. Through its regulatory oversight, the CFPB aims to safeguard consumers from unfair practices while enhancing trust and confidence in the mortgage lending system.

License Law and Regulation

Licensing Requirements for MLOs

In the realm of mortgage origination, the licensing requirements for individuals, particularly Mortgage Loan Originators (MLOs), are stringent and meticulously outlined to ensure the integrity and professionalism of the industry. The Secure and Fair Enforcement for Mortgage Licensing Act (SAFE Act) mandates that any individual engaging in the business of loan origination must obtain a license through the Nationwide Multistate Licensing System & Registry (NMLS). This requirement is pivotal for those who take applications or offer loan terms to consumers, as it serves to protect the public by ensuring that MLOs meet minimum standards for licensure.

To be eligible for licensure, candidates must fulfill several key criteria. Firstly, they are required to complete pre-licensure education courses approved by the NMLS. This education component consists of at least 20 hours of instruction, which covers federal law and regulation, ethics, including instruction on fraud, consumer protection, and fair lending issues, and lending standards for the nontraditional mortgage product marketplace.

Following the completion of education requirements, candidates must pass the SAFE MLO Test, which assesses their knowledge and comprehension of federal and state law and regulations, mortgage origination practices, and ethics. The test is designed to ensure that licensed MLOs possess the necessary competence and understanding to perform their duties ethically and effectively.

In addition to educational and examination requirements, the SAFE Act stipulates that MLOs must submit fingerprints to the NMLS for an FBI criminal background check. The purpose of this check is to identify any past criminal activity that might disqualify them from licensure. A clean criminal record is crucial, as certain felonies, especially those involving fraud, dishonesty, breach of trust, or money laundering, can render an individual ineligible for licensure.

Another critical aspect of the licensing process is the assessment of financial responsibility. MLOs must demonstrate a track record of financial integrity, which includes a review of their credit report. The absence of financial responsibility, evidenced by such issues as non-payment of judgments or tax liens, can be grounds for license denial.

Furthermore, the SAFE Act requires applicants to disclose any administrative, civil, or criminal findings against them, which are then carefully reviewed as part of the licensing process. This comprehensive vetting ensures that only individuals who have demonstrated ethical conduct and responsibility in their professional and personal lives are granted the privilege to serve as MLOs.

Once licensed, MLOs are assigned a unique identifier through the NMLS. This identifier must be provided to consumers and included in various documents, facilitating the tracking of their activities and compliance with federal and state regulations. The unique identifier also aids consumers in researching their MLO's history and standing, promoting transparency and trust in the mortgage origination process.

MLOs are required to renew their licenses annually, which includes completing continuing education requirements and updating their NMLS record with any changes to their personal or professional status. This ongoing education and reporting ensure that MLOs remain current with evolving laws, regulations, and best practices, further safeguarding consumers and maintaining the integrity of the mortgage industry.

The licensing of MLOs under the SAFE Act and through the NMLS is a critical component of the regulatory framework that governs the mortgage industry. It ensures that individuals involved in mortgage origination possess the necessary knowledge, ethical standards, and professionalism to provide consumers with responsible and compliant lending services.

MLO-Licensed Services Overview

In the realm of mortgage finance, Mortgage Loan Originators (MLOs) play a pivotal role, necessitating a comprehensive understanding of the services that require an MLO license. These services are critical to the mortgage process, ensuring that borrowers receive knowledgeable, ethical, and legally compliant assistance. The licensing of MLOs underlines the importance of these services in maintaining the integrity and functionality of the mortgage industry.

Loan Origination is the foundational service requiring an MLO license. This process involves taking a borrower's loan application, conducting initial assessments, and moving the application through to approval or denial. MLOs must be adept at evaluating the borrower's financial information, including income, assets, debts, and credit history, to determine eligibility for various loan products. The complexity of loan origination demands a thorough understanding of lending regulations, underwriting criteria, and the ability to accurately complete and process loan documentation.

Mortgage Advice is another critical service provided by licensed MLOs. This involves guiding borrowers through the maze of available loan options, interest rates, payment terms, and potential financial implications of their mortgage decisions. MLOs must possess a deep knowledge of the mortgage market, including federal and state regulations, to offer advice that aligns with the borrower's financial goals and circumstances. The advisory role extends to explaining the implications of different mortgage products, interest rates, and loan terms, ensuring borrowers make informed decisions.

Loan Structuring represents a specialized service that requires not only a license but also a high level of expertise. Structuring a loan involves tailoring the loan terms to meet the specific needs of the borrower while ensuring compliance with lending standards and regulations. This can include adjusting the loan amount, interest rate, repayment schedule, and other critical loan parameters. Effective loan structuring requires an MLO to balance the borrower's financial capabilities with the lender's risk management requirements, a task that demands both creativity and a comprehensive understanding of mortgage products.

Negotiations with Borrowers is a service that underscores the importance of communication skills and ethical considerations in the mortgage process. MLOs are often required to negotiate loan terms, interest rates, and closing costs on behalf of the lender or the borrower. This process requires a clear understanding of negotiation tactics, regulatory limits, and the ethical standards that govern mortgage lending. MLOs must navigate these negotiations with a focus on achieving outcomes that are fair, compliant with lending laws, and in the best interest of all parties involved.

Each of these services necessitates a license as they involve complex financial transactions, personal data handling, and significant legal responsibilities. The licensing process ensures that MLOs have the requisite knowledge, skills, and ethical grounding to perform these services effectively and legally. It also provides a mechanism for regulatory oversight, ensuring that MLOs adhere to industry standards and regulations designed to protect consumers and maintain the integrity of the mortgage lending process.

The requirement for MLOs to be licensed for these services is not merely a regulatory formality but a critical measure to ensure that borrowers receive competent, ethical, and professional assistance in navigating one of the most significant financial decisions of their lives. Through rigorous pre-licensure education, testing, and ongoing professional development, licensed MLOs are equipped to provide services that are essential to the functioning of the mortgage industry and the financial well-being of borrowers.

Allowable Activities Without MLO License

In the regulatory landscape of mortgage loan origination, certain roles and responsibilities can be performed without holding a Mortgage Loan Originator (MLO) license. Specifically, underwriters, clerical staff, and loan processors engage in critical yet distinct activities that support the mortgage process without necessitating direct interaction with borrowers in a capacity that would require licensure. Understanding these allowable activities sheds light on the operational framework within which these professionals operate, ensuring compliance with state and federal regulations.

Underwriters play a pivotal role in the mortgage approval process by assessing the creditworthiness of applicants. Their primary function involves evaluating the risk associated with lending to a particular borrower based on an analysis of credit reports, employment history, income, debt-to-income ratio, and other financial indicators. Underwriters do not engage directly with borrowers to negotiate loan terms or provide loan advice, which are activities reserved for licensed MLOs. Instead, they make decisions based on documented criteria and financial data to determine loan approval, conditions, or denials. Their work is crucial in maintaining the financial integrity of the lending process, ensuring loans are issued in accordance with lending standards and regulatory requirements.

Clerical staff in mortgage lending environments handle a variety of administrative tasks that support the loan origination process. These tasks may include data entry, document preparation and management, scheduling appointments, and maintaining records. Clerical staff do not make lending decisions, offer guidance on loan products, or engage in negotiations with borrowers. Their role is to provide organizational and administrative support, ensuring that loan files are complete, accurate, and processed efficiently. This support is essential for the smooth operation of lending institutions but does not require the staff to be licensed as MLOs since their activities do not involve direct financial advising or decision-making with respect to loan origination.

Loan processors bridge the gap between the loan application received by an MLO and the final decision made by an underwriter. They gather, organize, and verify all necessary documentation needed to support a loan application, such as employment verification, bank statements, and property appraisals. Loan processors ensure that the application package is comprehensive and ready for underwriting evaluation. While they may have direct communication with borrowers to request additional documentation or clarify information, they do not offer advice on loan terms or make decisions regarding loan approval. Their role is critical in preparing accurate and complete loan files for underwriting assessment, facilitating a timely and effective review process.

It is important to note that while these roles are exempt from MLO licensure requirements, professionals in these positions must still adhere to strict ethical standards and regulatory guidelines. They are expected to maintain confidentiality, demonstrate accuracy in their work, and operate within the legal framework established for the mortgage industry. Their contributions, while not requiring direct interaction with borrowers regarding loan advice or negotiation, are indispensable to the integrity and efficiency of the mortgage lending process.

Entities Requiring Licensed MLOs

In the realm of mortgage lending and origination, the requirement for licensed Mortgage Loan Originators (MLOs) is a critical component ensuring compliance, professionalism, and consumer protection within the industry. Entities such as mortgage brokers and non-depository lenders stand at the forefront of this requirement, necessitating a thorough understanding of their obligations under the Secure and Fair Enforcement for Mortgage Licensing Act (SAFE Act) and state-specific regulations. These entities play a pivotal role in the mortgage process, acting as intermediaries between borrowers and lenders, and their activities are subject to stringent regulatory oversight to maintain the integrity of the mortgage industry.

Mortgage brokers, by definition, are individuals or companies that act as intermediaries, facilitating the process of obtaining a mortgage for a borrower by sourcing loan options from various lenders. Given their role in advising on, applying for, and negotiating mortgage loans, brokers are required to have licensed MLOs within their teams. This licensing ensures that brokers possess the necessary knowledge and adhere to ethical standards when providing services to consumers. The licensing process for MLOs involves completing pre-licensure education, passing the NMLS exam, and submitting to background and credit checks, thereby ensuring that only qualified individuals engage in mortgage loan origination.

Non-depository lenders, which include entities that offer mortgage loans without accepting deposits from the public, also fall under the purview of entities requiring licensed MLOs. These lenders, often referred to as direct lenders, finance mortgage loans with their own capital or borrowed funds, making the role of a licensed MLO within these organizations crucial for assessing borrower eligibility, processing loan applications, and ensuring compliance with federal and state mortgage lending laws.

The SAFE Act and its implementing regulations provide a uniform framework for the licensing and registration of MLOs across the United States, aiming to enhance consumer protection and reduce fraud. This act mandates that MLOs employed by mortgage brokers and non-depository lenders must register with the Nationwide Mortgage Licensing System and Registry (NMLS), obtain a unique identifier, and maintain this registration annually. The act also stipulates continuing education requirements for MLOs, ensuring they remain knowledgeable about current laws, regulations, and best practices in the mortgage industry.

State-specific laws and regulations further detail the operational, licensing, and compliance requirements for entities employing MLOs. These regulations may include additional licensure requirements, higher education or experience thresholds, and more rigorous oversight of mortgage origination activities. It is incumbent upon mortgage brokers and non-depository lenders to not only ensure their MLOs are licensed but also to monitor compliance with ongoing education and regulatory updates pertinent to their state of operation.

The necessity for licensed MLOs within mortgage brokers and non-depository lenders underscores the importance of these roles in safeguarding the interests of borrowers and upholding the integrity of the mortgage lending process. Through rigorous licensing requirements and adherence to regulatory standards, these entities contribute to a transparent, fair, and ethical mortgage market, ultimately facilitating the goal of homeownership for consumers.

Exemptions for Depository Institutions

Federally insured depository institutions, including banks and credit unions, along with their employees, enjoy a specific exemption from the licensing requirements that are typically mandated for mortgage loan originators (MLOs) under the Secure and Fair Enforcement for Mortgage Licensing Act (SAFE Act). This exemption is rooted in the regulatory framework that governs these institutions, which is distinct from the oversight applied to non-depository mortgage lenders and brokers. The rationale behind this exemption lies in the comprehensive regulatory environment that already encompasses federally insured depository institutions, which includes rigorous oversight by federal banking regulators such as the Federal Reserve, the Office of the Comptroller of the Currency (OCC), and the National Credit Union Administration (NCUA).

The SAFE Act was enacted to enhance consumer protection and reduce fraud within the mortgage industry by establishing minimum standards for the licensing and registration of state-licensed mortgage loan originators. However, employees of federally insured depository institutions are subject to a different set of regulatory standards and oversight mechanisms, which are deemed to meet or exceed the consumer protection objectives of the SAFE Act. These employees are required to register with the Nationwide Mortgage Licensing System and Registry (NMLS), but they are not required to obtain licensure that state-licensed MLOs must secure. This registration process involves the submission of fingerprints for a background check, the provision of personal information for a public record, and the acquisition of a unique identifier through the NMLS. However, it stops short of the pre-licensure education, testing, and continuing education requirements that are obligatory for their counterparts in non-depository institutions.

Credit unions, being part of the cohort of federally insured depository institutions, also fall under this exemption. Despite their not-for-profit status, credit unions engage in mortgage lending activities under the same regulatory expectations and consumer protection mandates as banks, thereby negating the need for the additional layer of licensing required for MLOs in the broader market. The oversight by the NCUA, along with state credit union regulators, ensures that credit union employees engaged in mortgage lending adhere to high standards of professionalism and consumer protection.

It is important to note that while the SAFE Act exempts employees of federally insured depository institutions from its licensing requirements, it does not diminish the act's overarching goal of protecting consumers. Instead, it recognizes the existing regulatory frameworks that govern these institutions and their capacity to enforce standards of conduct and competence among their mortgage lending staff. This approach facilitates a streamlined regulatory environment that avoids duplicative oversight efforts while maintaining a robust consumer protection regime across all sectors of the mortgage industry.

The exemption of federally insured depository institutions and their employees from the SAFE Act's MLO licensing requirements underscores a tiered regulatory approach that balances the need for consumer protection with the recognition of existing federal oversight mechanisms. This exemption allows these institutions to focus on compliance with their primary regulators, ensuring that their mortgage lending activities are conducted in a manner that is safe, sound, and consistent with the best interests of consumers.

Licensee Qualifications & Application Process

Embarking on the path to becoming a licensed Mortgage Loan Originator (MLO) necessitates a comprehensive understanding of the qualifications and application process mandated by the Secure and Fair Enforcement for Mortgage Licensing Act (SAFE Act) and enforced through the Nationwide Mortgage Licensing System and Registry (NMLS). This process is designed to ensure that individuals entering this profession possess the requisite knowledge, integrity, and competence to perform their duties effectively, thereby safeguarding the interests of consumers and maintaining the integrity of the mortgage industry.

The initial step in this journey involves completing pre-license education, which is a critical component of the MLO licensing requirements. This education consists of 20 hours of coursework, covering topics such as federal law and regulations, ethics, lending standards for the nontraditional mortgage product marketplace, and an elective content area that provides a comprehensive overview of mortgage origination. It's imperative that the coursework is undertaken through an NMLS-approved course provider to ensure that it meets the regulatory standards and adequately prepares candidates for the challenges of the mortgage industry.

Following the completion of pre-license education, prospective MLOs must pass the SAFE MLO National Test with Uniform State Content. This examination assesses the candidate's knowledge and understanding of federal and state mortgage laws, evaluating their readiness to operate within the legal and regulatory framework governing the mortgage industry. Achieving a passing score on this exam is a testament to the candidate's proficiency in the key areas of mortgage law and ethics, signifying their preparedness to uphold the standards of practice required of a licensed MLO.

Background checks constitute another pivotal aspect of the MLO licensing process, encompassing a comprehensive review of the candidate's criminal history, credit report, and any previous financial regulatory actions against them. This scrutiny is intended to identify any past behaviors that might disqualify an individual from obtaining licensure, such as a history of fraud, money laundering, or other financial crimes. The SAFE Act specifically disallows licensure for individuals convicted of a felony involving fraud, dishonesty, breach of trust, or money laundering within the past seven years, or at any time if the felony involved a mortgage or real estate transaction.

In addition to these requirements, candidates must also submit fingerprints for a federal criminal background check and authorize the NMLS to obtain an independent credit report. These steps are crucial for assessing the candidate's financial responsibility and integrity, ensuring that those entering the profession are worthy of the trust placed in them by consumers and the industry at large.

The application process itself is facilitated through the NMLS, requiring candidates to provide detailed personal information, educational history, and employment records. This information is meticulously reviewed to verify the accuracy of the application and to ensure compliance with all regulatory requirements. Upon successful completion of all pre-licensure requirements, candidates are granted an MLO license, which must be renewed annually through the NMLS. This renewal process includes the completion of continuing education, which consists of eight hours of NMLS-approved coursework designed to keep MLOs abreast of the latest developments in mortgage laws, regulations, and best practices.

It's important to note that the qualifications and application process for MLO licensure are not merely bureaucratic hurdles but are foundational elements that ensure the professionalism, competence, and ethical conduct of those entering this critical field. By adhering to these stringent requirements, the mortgage industry strives to protect consumers, promote fairness in lending, and maintain the integrity of the mortgage finance system.

Test Retake Waiting Periods

The National Mortgage Licensing System (NMLS) mandates specific waiting periods for retaking the SAFE MLO Exam to ensure that candidates have ample time to prepare adequately for their next attempt. After the initial failure of the SAFE MLO Exam, candidates are required to wait a mandatory period of **30 days** before they can retake the exam. This waiting period applies to the first three unsuccessful attempts.

Should a candidate not pass the exam after these initial three attempts, a more extended waiting period is enforced. Specifically, candidates must then wait **180 days** before attempting the exam again. This extended waiting period applies to any subsequent attempts following the third unsuccessful try.

These waiting periods are designed to serve multiple purposes. Firstly, they provide candidates with a significant interval to review the exam content thoroughly, address any areas of weakness, and enhance their understanding of the material. This preparation is crucial for improving the likelihood of success in future attempts. Secondly, the waiting periods help to maintain the integrity and the rigorous standards of the licensing process, ensuring that all licensed Mortgage Loan Originators have demonstrated the requisite knowledge and competency in their field.

Candidates are encouraged to utilize this time effectively, focusing on areas of the exam content where they previously struggled. Engaging in additional study, taking advantage of preparatory courses, and utilizing practice exams are recommended strategies during these intervals. These actions not only aid in reinforcing the candidate's knowledge base but also in building confidence for future exam attempts.

It is essential for candidates to plan their study schedule and exam retakes carefully, considering these mandatory waiting periods. Adequate preparation and strategic planning are key to navigating the retake process successfully and achieving a passing score on the SAFE MLO Exam.

Sponsorship Requirement for MLOs

The sponsorship requirement for Mortgage Loan Originators (MLOs) is a pivotal aspect of the regulatory framework established under the Secure and Fair Enforcement for Mortgage

Licensing Act (SAFE Act) and enforced through the Nationwide Mortgage Licensing System and Registry (NMLS). This mandate necessitates that MLOs be sponsored by a licensed or registered entity, such as a mortgage broker, bank, credit union, or other financial institution, to maintain an active license and engage in the practice of loan origination. The essence of this requirement lies in ensuring that MLOs operate within a structured and accountable environment, fostering professionalism, compliance, and ethical conduct in the mortgage industry.

To comprehend the significance of the sponsorship requirement, it is essential to understand the role of a sponsor. A sponsor is a licensed or registered entity that assumes responsibility for the MLO's compliance with federal and state mortgage lending laws and regulations. The sponsor provides oversight, support, and guidance, ensuring that the MLO adheres to the highest standards of practice. This relationship is not merely administrative but is fundamentally rooted in the principles of accountability and integrity, serving as a safeguard against malpractice and enhancing consumer protection in the mortgage lending process.

The process of obtaining sponsorship involves several critical steps. Initially, an MLO must secure employment or an association with a licensed or registered entity willing to act as their sponsor. This entity must then register its sponsorship of the MLO with the NMLS, formally linking the MLO's license to the sponsoring entity. This linkage is crucial as it enables regulatory bodies to monitor the MLO's activities, ensuring compliance with licensing requirements and facilitating the oversight of mortgage origination practices.

The sponsorship requirement also plays a vital role in the professional development of MLOs. Through their association with a sponsoring entity, MLOs gain access to valuable resources, including training programs, compliance tools, and industry insights, which are instrumental in fostering their growth and expertise in the field. This symbiotic relationship enhances the MLO's ability to serve the needs of consumers effectively, offering informed advice, competitive loan options, and a streamlined origination process.

Moreover, the sponsorship requirement underscores the collective responsibility of the mortgage industry to uphold ethical standards and protect consumers. By mandating that MLOs be sponsored by licensed or registered entities, the regulatory framework ensures that individuals engaged in loan origination are not only qualified but are also aligned with the ethical and operational standards set forth by the industry. This alignment is critical in maintaining consumer trust and confidence in the mortgage lending process, which is foundational to the stability and integrity of the housing market.

The sponsorship requirement for MLOs serves as a fundamental element of the regulatory framework that governs the mortgage industry. It ensures that MLOs operate within a framework of accountability, receive ongoing support and guidance, and contribute to the ethical and professional conduct of mortgage lending. Entities sponsoring MLOs play a crucial role in enforcing compliance, fostering professional development, and safeguarding consumer interests, thereby enhancing the overall quality and integrity of mortgage loan origination.

Definition of MLO

A Mortgage Loan Originator (MLO) plays a pivotal role in the mortgage industry, acting as a crucial intermediary between potential borrowers and financial institutions offering mortgage loans. This professional is tasked with the responsibility of guiding applicants through the process of applying for a mortgage, providing them with a comprehensive understanding of the various loan options available, and assisting them in selecting the most suitable mortgage based on their financial situation and housing needs. The definition of an MLO extends beyond merely taking applications; it encompasses a broad spectrum of activities aimed at facilitating the successful acquisition of mortgage financing for the consumer.

At the core of an MLO's responsibilities is the ability to offer loan terms tailored to the borrower's financial circumstances. This involves a detailed analysis of the applicant's financial health, including income, debt levels, credit history, and savings, to determine their borrowing capacity. An MLO must possess a deep understanding of the mortgage products available in the market, including fixed-rate mortgages, adjustable-rate mortgages (ARMs), government-backed loans such as FHA, VA, and USDA loans, as well as jumbo loans and other non-conforming loan products. This knowledge enables the MLO to present the borrower with loan options that align with their long-term financial goals and housing needs.

Negotiation is another critical function of an MLO. This aspect of the role involves working with underwriters and lenders to secure favorable loan terms for the client. It may include negotiating interest rates, loan repayment terms, and closing costs. The MLO acts as the borrower's advocate, striving to achieve the best possible financial arrangement that ensures affordability and meets the lender's criteria for loan approval.

Assisting consumers in obtaining mortgages is a comprehensive duty that requires MLOs to be well-versed in the application process, from initial inquiry to closing. They must accurately gather and process personal and financial information from applicants, ensuring that all documentation is complete and complies with lending standards. MLOs are also responsible for explaining the legal and financial implications of the mortgage agreement to the borrower, ensuring they fully understand their obligations under the loan contract.

Furthermore, MLOs play a significant role in ensuring compliance with federal and state regulations governing mortgage lending. This includes adhering to laws such as the Truth in Lending Act (TILA), the Real Estate Settlement Procedures Act (RESPA), and the Equal Credit Opportunity Act (ECOA), among others. Compliance is critical to protect consumers from discriminatory lending practices and to ensure transparency throughout the mortgage process.

The role of a Mortgage Loan Originator (MLO) is complex, necessitating a combination of financial expertise, knowledge of the market, negotiation abilities, and a strong dedication to consumer protection and adherence to regulations. MLOs play a vital part in the mortgage lending process, offering the necessary expertise and guidance to manage the intricate aspects of mortgage financing. Their efforts ensure that borrowers are adequately informed, treated fairly, and able to obtain mortgage loans that align with their financial circumstances, thus facilitating their pursuit of homeownership.

Grounds for Denying a License

The process of obtaining a license as a Mortgage Loan Originator (MLO) is stringent and comprehensive, designed to ensure that individuals entering this profession meet the highest standards of integrity, competence, and professionalism. A critical aspect of this process involves understanding the grounds upon which an application for licensure can be denied. These grounds are primarily centered around protecting the public by ensuring that only qualified and trustworthy individuals are granted the privilege to operate within the mortgage industry.

Felony Convictions: One of the most straightforward grounds for denial is a history of felony convictions. The SAFE Act explicitly prohibits the issuance of an MLO license to any individual convicted of a felony involving fraud, dishonesty, breach of trust, or money laundering. Furthermore, if the conviction has occurred within the past seven years for any felony, the applicant is also ineligible for licensure. This strict criterion underscores the importance of moral character in the profession, reflecting the significant trust placed in MLOs by consumers and the financial system.

Financial Irresponsibility: Financial irresponsibility, manifesting through scenarios such as personal bankruptcy, a history of writing bad checks, or consistently failing to meet personal financial obligations, can also be a basis for license denial. This criterion is based on the premise that individuals who cannot manage their finances may not be suitable to advise others on financial matters, particularly in the context of significant transactions like mortgages.

False Application Information: Integrity in the application process is paramount. Providing false, misleading, or incomplete information during the licensure application process is a serious offense that can lead to the denial of a license. This includes falsification of educational achievements, hiding previous criminal convictions, or lying about financial status. The requirement for honesty in the application process ensures that the regulatory bodies can make informed decisions based on accurate and verifiable information.

Failure to Meet SAFE Act Standards: The SAFE Act sets forth a variety of standards that applicants must meet, including educational requirements, passing a comprehensive national test with a uniform state component, and completing pre-licensure and continuing education courses. Failure to meet any of these standards, such as not achieving the required score on the national test or not completing the necessary education credits, constitutes grounds for denying a license. These standards are in place to ensure that all MLOs have the requisite knowledge and skills to perform their duties effectively and ethically.

The denial of an MLO license can occur due to felony convictions, financial irresponsibility, the provision of false application information, or failure to meet the standards established by the SAFE Act. This highlights the stringent vetting process aimed at maintaining the integrity and professionalism of the mortgage industry. Such criteria are essential in ensuring that those who receive licensure are qualified, reliable, and capable of delivering the highest standard of service to both consumers and the industry as a whole.

License Maintenance Essentials

Maintaining an active Mortgage Loan Originator (MLO) license requires adherence to specific renewal and continuing education requirements, as well as understanding the conditions under which one must retake the SAFE MLO National Test with Uniform State Content. These components are critical for ensuring that MLOs remain compliant with regulatory standards and are equipped with the latest knowledge and skills necessary for their profession.

Renewal Period: The renewal of an MLO license typically occurs on an annual basis, with the specific period and deadlines varying by state. Licensees must submit a renewal application through the Nationwide Multistate Licensing System and Registry (NMLS) by the designated deadline, usually by the end of the year, to avoid lapses in licensure. It is imperative for MLOs to monitor their state's renewal schedule and requirements closely to ensure timely compliance.

Continuing Education Requirements: To qualify for license renewal, MLOs must complete a minimum of eight hours of continuing education (CE) annually. This education must include three hours of federal law and regulations, two hours of ethics (which should cover fraud, consumer protection, and fair lending issues), and two hours of training related to lending standards for the nontraditional mortgage product marketplace. Additionally, one hour must be dedicated to elective education that pertains to mortgage origination. Some states may have specific requirements beyond the federal minimum, including education on state-specific laws and practices. MLOs should verify their state's unique CE requirements to ensure full compliance.

Maintaining Active License: Active licensure signifies that an MLO has met all renewal requirements, including CE credits, and has no outstanding compliance issues. An active license is essential for engaging in MLO activities legally. Failure to renew the license or complete the required CE can result in the license being placed in an inactive status, prohibiting the MLO from conducting loan origination activities until all reinstatement criteria are met.

Retaking the SAFE MLO National Test with Uniform State Content: If an MLO's license becomes inactive for a period specified by their state's regulations, typically for failing to renew the license or complete CE requirements, the individual may be required to retake and pass the SAFE MLO National Test with Uniform State Content to reactivate the license. This requirement is designed to ensure that returning MLOs possess current knowledge of mortgage laws, regulations, and best practices. The specifics of this requirement, including the inactivity period after which retaking the test is necessary, can vary by state. Therefore, MLOs should familiarize themselves with their state's policies regarding license inactivity and test retake requirements.

Maintaining an MLO license demands careful attention to renewal deadlines, diligent completion of continuing education, and adherence to state-specific requirements. These measures ensure that MLOs remain competent and compliant professionals within the mortgage industry, capable of providing high-quality services to consumers.

NMLS Employment & Identifier Requirements

Navigating the Nationwide Multistate Licensing System & Registry (NMLS) requirements is a fundamental aspect of maintaining compliance as a Mortgage Loan Originator (MLO). The NMLS platform serves as a comprehensive database for licensing and registration information, facilitating transparency and accountability within the mortgage industry. Among the critical NMLS requirements are change of employment notifications, required submissions/disclosures, and NMLS identifier requirements, each of which plays a vital role in the regulatory landscape.

Change of employment notifications are essential for ensuring that the NMLS registry remains up-to-date with an MLO's current employment status. When an MLO changes employers, they must promptly update their NMLS record to reflect this change. This process involves submitting a new MU4 form through the NMLS, which captures the MLO's employment history, background checks, and other pertinent information. The timely update of employment information is not just a regulatory requirement; it also supports the integrity of the mortgage industry by providing accurate, current data on MLOs to regulators, employers, and the public.

Required submissions and disclosures form another cornerstone of NMLS compliance. MLOs are required to submit a range of documents and information through the NMLS, including but not limited to personal history and experience, financial responsibility, and criminal background checks. Additionally, disclosures related to any administrative, civil, or criminal findings against the MLO must be reported. These submissions are critical for the licensing process, as they allow regulatory bodies to assess the suitability and eligibility of individuals to operate within the mortgage industry. The NMLS facilitates these submissions electronically, streamlining the process and ensuring a central repository for all relevant information.

The NMLS identifier requirements mandate that every MLO is assigned a unique identifier upon registration. This unique identifier must be included on all loan applications, advertisements, and other communications with consumers. The purpose of the NMLS identifier is multifold: it enhances transparency, enables consumers to research the licensing status and history of MLOs, and aids in the tracking of MLO activity across state lines. The consistent use of the NMLS identifier in all professional activities helps to build trust with consumers by reinforcing the MLO's accountability and adherence to regulatory standards.

Compliance with these NMLS requirements is not merely a matter of fulfilling legal obligations; it is integral to the professional conduct and ethical responsibility of every MLO. The NMLS platform provides a centralized, standardized framework for managing these requirements, thereby supporting the overall goal of promoting integrity, transparency, and trust in the mortgage industry. As such, MLOs must remain diligent in their understanding and application of NMLS requirements, ensuring that their actions align with both the letter and the spirit of the law.

Temporary Authority for MLOs

The Economic Growth, Regulatory Relief, and Consumer Protection Act, enacted in May 2018, introduced a provision granting **Temporary Authority to Originate** (TAO) for Mortgage Loan Originators (MLOs). This provision significantly impacts MLOs in transition—whether moving between states or changing employers—by allowing them to continue originating loans while awaiting the approval of their new license. This legislative change aims to streamline the licensing process, reduce employment gaps for MLOs, and maintain a steady flow of mortgage lending activities without compromising consumer protection or regulatory compliance.

Under the TAO, an MLO who is already licensed in one state can obtain temporary authority to operate in another state where they have applied for licensure. Similarly, MLOs who are transitioning between employers within the same state can also benefit from this temporary authority while their new license application is processed. The temporary authority period lasts for 120 days, providing a substantial window to ensure that the licensing process does not disrupt the MLO's ability to work.

To qualify for **Temporary Authority to Originate**, an MLO must meet specific criteria:

1. **Application Submission**: The MLO must have submitted a complete application for licensure in the new state or with the new employer. This includes all required fees, background checks, and any other documentation requested by the state regulator.

2. **Current Licensure**: The MLO must hold a valid MLO license in another state. This ensures that only those with a proven track record and existing regulatory approval can benefit from temporary authority.

3. **No Disqualifying Events**: The MLO must not have any disqualifying events, such as revocation of a previous license, criminal convictions related to financial crimes, or any other actions that would preclude them from obtaining a mortgage license under state or federal law.

The introduction of TAO represents a significant regulatory adjustment designed to support career mobility for MLOs while maintaining rigorous oversight of mortgage lending practices. It acknowledges the dynamic nature of the mortgage industry and the need for regulatory frameworks that support rather than hinder professional transitions.

For regulatory bodies, the TAO necessitates robust systems for tracking applications and ensuring that MLOs operating under temporary authority comply with all relevant laws and regulations. State agencies must coordinate closely with the Nationwide Multistate Licensing System and Registry (NMLS) to monitor the status of applications and enforce compliance.

For MLOs, understanding the nuances of TAO is crucial. They must ensure that their application for licensure in the new state is complete and submitted promptly. They should also be aware of the 120-day limit on temporary authority and plan accordingly to avoid any lapse in their ability to legally originate loans. MLOs must also remain vigilant about their compliance obligations, as the temporary authority does not exempt them from adhering to state-specific laws and regulations governing mortgage origination.

In practice, the TAO facilitates a smoother transition for MLOs, reducing employment interruptions and allowing for continued professional growth. However, it places a premium on the MLO's responsibility to manage their licensure status proactively and maintain the highest standards of ethical conduct and compliance. This balance between regulatory flexibility and strict adherence to consumer protection standards underscores the dual priorities of the Economic Growth, Regulatory Relief, and Consumer Protection Act: facilitating economic activity while safeguarding the integrity of the mortgage lending process.

Compliance

Regulator's Authority to Audit and Interview

State regulators wield comprehensive authority to ensure compliance with mortgage lending laws and regulations, safeguarding the integrity of the mortgage industry and protecting consumer interests. This authority encompasses the power to conduct thorough examinations of a licensee's books, records, and any other documents pertinent to the mortgage lending process. Such examinations are crucial for verifying that Mortgage Loan Originators (MLOs) and their affiliated entities adhere to state and federal regulations, including but not limited to the Truth in Lending Act (TILA), Real Estate Settlement Procedures Act (RESPA), and the Secure and Fair Enforcement for Mortgage Licensing Act (SAFE Act).

The scope of these examinations can vary but typically includes a detailed review of loan documentation, advertising materials, compensation agreements, and consumer disclosures. Regulators aim to identify any discrepancies, misrepresentations, or violations of lending laws that could harm consumers or undermine the fairness of the mortgage market. This process is not limited to a superficial review; it involves a deep dive into the operational practices of the licensee to ensure that all aspects of mortgage origination, processing, underwriting, and closing are conducted in compliance with legal standards.

In addition to reviewing documents, state regulators also possess the authority to interview employees at all levels within a mortgage origination company. These interviews can be instrumental in uncovering practices that may not be immediately apparent through document reviews alone. Employees might provide insights into the company's procedures, culture, and compliance efforts, offering regulators a more comprehensive understanding of the licensee's operations. This direct engagement allows regulators to assess the practical application of policies and procedures related to mortgage lending and consumer protection.

The authority to audit and interview is not arbitrarily exercised; it is a targeted effort to address specific areas of concern, such as compliance with anti-discrimination laws, accuracy of loan disclosures, and the handling of consumer complaints. When consumer complaints are received, they often trigger a more focused examination of the licensee's practices related to the issues raised in the complaints. This ensures that consumer protection remains at the forefront of regulatory efforts, with swift action taken to rectify any identified problems.

Regulatory examinations and interviews are conducted with the dual objectives of enforcement and education. While the primary goal is to identify and correct violations, regulators also use these opportunities to provide guidance to licensees on how to improve their compliance programs and better serve consumers. This approach underscores the regulatory commitment to not only enforce the law but also to promote best practices within the mortgage industry.

The power of state regulators to audit records and interview employees is a critical component of the regulatory framework that governs the mortgage industry. It ensures that licensees operate with transparency, accountability, and a steadfast commitment to consumer protection. By maintaining rigorous oversight of mortgage lending practices, state regulators play a pivotal role in upholding the integrity of the mortgage market and fostering trust among consumers, lenders, and other stakeholders in the real estate finance ecosystem.

Prohibited Acts in Real Estate Transactions

In the realm of mortgage loan origination, adherence to ethical standards and regulatory compliance is paramount. Among the practices strictly prohibited are paying for real estate agent advertisements, using a supervisor's NMLS unique identifier, and omitting debt from a credit report. Each of these actions not only undermines the integrity of the mortgage process but also violates federal and state laws, leading to significant legal and professional consequences.

Paying for Real Estate Agent Ads: Mortgage Loan Originators (MLOs) are prohibited from paying for advertising services on behalf of real estate agents. This prohibition is designed to prevent conflicts of interest and ensure that recommendations for mortgage loan origination services are based on merit and not on financial incentives. Such practices could mislead consumers and distort the market, compromising the fairness and transparency essential to the mortgage industry. Regulatory bodies view the payment for real estate agent advertisements as an unethical kickback or referral fee, which is explicitly forbidden under the Real Estate Settlement Procedures Act (RESPA).

Using Supervisor's NMLS Unique Identifier: The Nationwide Multistate Licensing System & Registry (NMLS) assigns a unique identifier to each licensed MLO. This identifier serves as a professional fingerprint, linking the MLO to their licensing information, disciplinary history, and compliance records. Using a supervisor's NMLS unique identifier, or any identifier other than one's own, constitutes a serious breach of regulatory standards. It misrepresents the identity of the loan originator involved in a mortgage transaction, thereby misleading consumers and regulators. Such an act undermines the accountability and transparency that the NMLS unique identifier system is designed to ensure.

Omitting Debt from a Credit Report: Integrity in representing a borrower's financial situation is a cornerstone of mortgage loan origination. Omitting debt from a credit report is a deceptive practice that distorts a borrower's creditworthiness and risk profile. Accurate disclosure of debt is critical for assessing the borrower's ability to repay the loan, a fundamental aspect of responsible lending. Omitting debt not only violates the ethical standards expected of MLOs but also contravenes the Truth in Lending Act (TILA) and the Dodd-Frank Wall Street Reform and Consumer Protection Act, both of which mandate truthful, fair, and transparent lending practices.

Violations of these prohibitions can result in severe penalties, including fines, revocation of the MLO's license, and potential criminal charges. Moreover, such actions can tarnish the professional reputation of the MLO, leading to loss of credibility and trust with clients and within the industry. To maintain compliance and uphold the integrity of the mortgage process, MLOs must rigorously adhere to all regulatory guidelines and ethical standards, ensuring that their practices reflect the principles of honesty, transparency, and fairness.

Required Conduct in Complaint Investigations

In the realm of mortgage loan origination, adherence to regulatory compliance is paramount. Mortgage Loan Originators (MLOs) are obligated to engage in certain conduct that ensures transparency, accountability, and the safeguarding of consumer interests. This includes the provision of documents during complaint investigations, the retention of records, and the furnishing of these records to state regulators upon request.

Providing Documents in Complaint Investigations

When a complaint is lodged against an MLO or their associated entity, it is imperative that all requested documents are provided promptly to the investigating authority. This may include, but is not limited to, loan application files, communication records between the MLO and the consumer, and any other documentation relevant to the complaint. Failure to provide these documents can lead to regulatory penalties, including fines and, in severe cases, revocation of licensure.

Record Retention

MLOs must adhere to strict guidelines regarding the retention of records. Federal and state laws dictate the minimum period for which records must be kept, typically ranging from two to five years, depending on the nature of the document. This includes records of transactions, correspondence with consumers, disclosures provided to consumers, and any other documents that substantiate compliance with applicable laws and regulations. Effective record retention policies not only facilitate compliance with legal obligations but also enable MLOs to defend against complaints or allegations of non-compliance.

Providing Records to State Regulators

State regulators have the authority to request access to an MLO's records as part of routine examinations or investigations. MLOs are required to comply with these requests in a timely and complete manner. This may involve submitting copies of requested documents or allowing regulators to inspect records at the MLO's place of business. The ability to quickly and accurately provide these records is indicative of an MLO's commitment to regulatory compliance and can significantly impact the outcome of regulatory examinations or investigations.

The required conduct of providing documents in complaint investigations, retaining records appropriately, and supplying records to state regulators is critical for maintaining compliance within the mortgage industry. These practices not only protect consumers but also uphold the integrity of the mortgage lending process. MLOs must establish and follow rigorous policies and procedures to ensure that they can meet these obligations effectively and efficiently.

Assumable Loan Scenarios and Conditions

Assumable loans present a unique opportunity in the mortgage landscape, allowing a new borrower to take over the existing loan terms of a seller's mortgage, subject to lender approval. This process can be particularly attractive in an environment where interest rates are rising, as it enables the new borrower to benefit from the seller's existing lower interest rate. However, the assumption of a mortgage is not a straightforward transaction and is contingent upon several critical conditions and the lender's explicit consent.

The primary condition for an assumable loan scenario is the type of loan. Generally, loans insured by the Federal Housing Administration (FHA), U.S. Department of Veterans Affairs (VA), and U.S. Department of Agriculture (USDA) are assumable, while conventional loans are not, unless they explicitly state otherwise. The new borrower must qualify under the lender's criteria, which typically involves creditworthiness assessment, debt-to-income ratio evaluation, and sometimes, the payment of an assumption fee.

The lender's role in this process is pivotal. Upon receiving a request for loan assumption, the lender will review the new borrower's application in much the same way as an original loan application. This includes a thorough examination of the borrower's financial stability, employment history, credit score, and other factors that demonstrate the ability to maintain mortgage payments. The lender's approval is not guaranteed and hinges on the new borrower meeting specific lending criteria that may mirror or exceed the original loan's requirements.

Moreover, the lender will assess the loan's current standing, ensuring that the mortgage is not in default and that the assumption does not contravene any existing loan agreements. If the lender approves the assumption, legal documentation is prepared to transfer the obligation from the seller to the buyer, effectively making the new borrower responsible for the remaining mortgage payments.

It's also worth noting that while the assumption process can offer benefits, such as avoiding closing costs associated with a new mortgage, it requires meticulous consideration of all legal and financial implications. Both the seller and the prospective buyer must understand their rights and obligations under the loan assumption agreement to ensure a smooth transition and continued compliance with the mortgage terms.

Permissible MLO Activities

Mortgage Loan Originators (MLOs) play a pivotal role in guiding consumers through the complex process of obtaining a mortgage. Their responsibilities are not only to facilitate the transaction but also to ensure that borrowers are well-informed and receive fair treatment throughout the process. In compliance with federal and state regulations, MLOs are permitted to engage in a variety of activities that support these objectives.

One of the primary permissible activities of MLOs is assisting borrowers with the mortgage application process. This involves gathering necessary documentation from the borrower, including financial statements, employment verification, and any other relevant information that supports the borrower's application. MLOs must ensure that the application is completed accurately and thoroughly, as this is critical for underwriting decisions. They must also be adept at using the Nationwide Multistate Licensing System and Registry (NMLS) to submit applications and track their progress.

Providing loan disclosures is another critical activity that MLOs are authorized to perform. Federal laws, such as the Truth in Lending Act (TILA) and the Real Estate Settlement Procedures Act (RESPA), mandate the delivery of specific disclosures at various stages of the mortgage process. These disclosures include, but are not limited to, the Loan Estimate and the Closing Disclosure, which detail the terms of the loan, including interest rates, fees, and other costs associated with the mortgage. MLOs must ensure that these disclosures are provided to the borrower in a timely manner, allowing them to make informed decisions about their loan options.

Advising on mortgage products is also within the scope of permissible activities for MLOs. This involves analyzing the borrower's financial situation, including their income, debts, and credit history, to determine which mortgage products best suit their needs. MLOs must have a thorough understanding of various mortgage products, including fixed-rate mortgages, adjustable-rate mortgages (ARMs), government-backed loans such as FHA, VA, and USDA loans, as well as non-conventional loans. They must be able to explain the features, benefits, and potential drawbacks of each option, helping borrowers to navigate the complexities of mortgage financing.

Furthermore, MLOs are allowed to provide guidance on interest rates and lock-in options. They can explain how interest rates are determined, the impact of market conditions on rates, and the benefits and risks associated with locking in an interest rate. This guidance is crucial for borrowers to understand how interest rates affect the overall cost of their loan and their monthly payments.

In fulfilling these permissible activities, MLOs must always act in the best interest of the borrower, maintaining transparency and avoiding any actions that could be construed as misleading or coercive. They must adhere to ethical standards and regulatory requirements, ensuring that their advice and assistance contribute to a fair and equitable mortgage lending process.

Penalties for Noncompliance

Mortgage Loan Originators (MLOs) operate within a tightly regulated environment, where adherence to the Secure and Fair Enforcement for Mortgage Licensing Act (SAFE Act) and state regulatory standards is not just encouraged but mandated. The consequences of noncompliance are severe and multifaceted, designed to underscore the importance of these regulations in maintaining the integrity of the mortgage industry and protecting consumers. Penalties for failing to conduct certain duties range from financial fines to the suspension or revocation of licenses, each carrying significant implications for the MLO's professional standing and operational capabilities.

Financial fines are often the first line of disciplinary action for noncompliance. These fines are not arbitrary but are calculated based on the severity and frequency of the infractions. They serve a dual purpose: penalizing the offending MLO while also acting as a deterrent against future violations. The exact amount can vary widely, depending on the specific nature of the noncompliance and the jurisdiction in which the MLO operates. In some cases, fines can escalate to substantial sums, particularly for violations that result in significant consumer harm or demonstrate a pattern of reckless or negligent behavior.

License suspension presents a more severe penalty, directly impacting the MLO's ability to conduct business. During the suspension period, the MLO is prohibited from engaging in any activities that require a license under the SAFE Act. This not only halts the MLO's current operations but can also have lasting effects on their professional reputation and relationships with clients and lenders. The length of the suspension can vary, often depending on the MLO's willingness to address the violations and take corrective actions.

Revocation of an MLO's license is the most severe penalty and is generally reserved for the most egregious or repeated violations. License revocation is effectively a professional banishment, stripping the MLO of the legal authority to practice within the industry. This penalty is not imposed lightly and usually follows a comprehensive investigation and a finding of significant or repeated noncompliance. Once revoked, an MLO may face substantial hurdles to re-enter the industry, including waiting periods, re-education, and re-examination requirements, if reinstatement is even possible.

The imposition of these penalties is not just about punishing individual MLOs but also about upholding the standards of the mortgage industry as a whole. Regulatory bodies, such as the Consumer Financial Protection Bureau (CFPB) and state licensing agencies, are tasked with enforcing these standards and have broad authority to investigate complaints, audit records, and take disciplinary action against noncompliant MLOs. Their goal is to ensure that the mortgage market operates fairly, transparently, and efficiently, with a strong emphasis on consumer protection.

In addition to these direct penalties, MLOs may also face indirect consequences, such as damage to their professional reputation, loss of business, and legal challenges from affected consumers. The cumulative effect of these penalties and consequences underscores the critical importance of compliance within the mortgage industry. MLOs must therefore be diligent in their adherence to the SAFE Act and state regulatory standards, not only to avoid penalties but also to maintain the trust and confidence of their clients and the public.

General Loan Origination Scenarios

The loan origination process is a comprehensive procedure that involves multiple steps, each critical to the successful issuance of a mortgage loan. This process begins with the loan inquiry and application, moves through documentation and verification, and culminates in the closing and funding of the loan. Throughout these stages, Mortgage Loan Originators (MLOs) must adhere to a strict regulatory framework to ensure compliance and protect the interests of the borrower.

Loan Inquiry and Application: The first step in the loan origination process is the loan inquiry, where potential borrowers contact an MLO to discuss loan options. During this phase, MLOs provide information on different mortgage products and the qualifications for each. Once a borrower decides to proceed, they complete a loan application, providing personal and financial information, including income, employment history, assets, and liabilities. MLOs are responsible for ensuring the application is filled out accurately and completely.

Documentation and Verification: After the application is submitted, the MLO collects necessary documentation to verify the information provided by the borrower. This includes tax returns, pay stubs, bank statements, and other financial documents. The MLO must also order a credit report to assess the borrower's creditworthiness. Throughout this process, MLOs must comply with the Equal Credit Opportunity Act (ECOA) and the Fair Credit Reporting Act (FCRA), ensuring that all applicants are treated fairly and that their privacy is protected.

Disclosure Delivery: Early in the application process, MLOs are required to provide borrowers with several disclosures, including the Loan Estimate, which outlines the estimated costs associated with the loan. This disclosure is mandated by the Truth in Lending Act (TILA) and must be delivered within three business days of the loan application. The Loan Estimate helps borrowers understand the costs of their loan, including interest rates, monthly payments, and closing costs.

Underwriting: Once the documentation is collected and verified, the loan application moves to underwriting. During this phase, underwriters review the application, documentation, and credit report to assess the risk of lending to the borrower. They confirm that the borrower meets all the lender's criteria and that the loan complies with all applicable laws and regulations. The underwriter also evaluates the property's value and condition through an appraisal report.

MLO Compliance Checkpoints: Throughout the loan origination process, MLOs must adhere to various compliance checkpoints. These include ensuring accurate and timely disclosures, protecting borrower information per the Gramm-Leach-Bliley Act (GLBA), and adhering to anti-discrimination laws under ECOA. MLOs must also comply with the Secure and Fair Enforcement for Mortgage Licensing Act (SAFE Act) by maintaining their license and registration through the Nationwide Multistate Licensing System and Registry (NMLS).

Closing and Funding: The final step in the loan origination process is the closing, where the loan is finalized, and funds are disbursed. The borrower and MLO review the Closing Disclosure, which provides the final loan terms and closing costs, ensuring accuracy and compliance with the Loan Estimate. After all documents are signed and the closing conditions are met, the loan is funded, and the borrower becomes responsible for repayment according to the loan terms.

Throughout each of these stages, MLOs play a pivotal role in guiding borrowers through the complex mortgage process, ensuring compliance with federal and state regulations, and facilitating the successful funding of loans. Their adherence to compliance checkpoints and regulatory standards is essential for protecting consumers and maintaining the integrity of the mortgage lending industry.

NMLS Identifier in Advertising

In the realm of mortgage loan origination, the inclusion of the Nationwide Multistate Licensing System (NMLS) unique identifier in advertisements is not merely a suggestion but a stringent regulatory requirement. This mandate serves multiple critical functions, primarily aimed at enhancing transparency, accountability, and consumer protection within the mortgage industry. The NMLS unique identifier is a permanent number assigned to each mortgage loan originator (MLO) upon successful registration with the NMLS. This identifier must be conspicuously displayed in all forms of advertising, including but not limited to print, digital, and broadcast media.

The requirement for MLOs to include their NMLS unique identifier in advertisements is grounded in the Secure and Fair Enforcement for Mortgage Licensing Act (SAFE Act), which aims to improve the integrity of the mortgage industry and facilitate consumers' ability to identify and verify the licensure status of mortgage professionals with whom they consider doing business. By incorporating the NMLS unique identifier, advertisements provide a direct link to the NMLS Consumer Access website, where consumers can access comprehensive information regarding the licensing and professional history of MLOs. This level of transparency empowers consumers to make informed decisions and fosters a culture of trust and accountability in the mortgage lending process.

Failure to comply with this requirement can result in significant repercussions for MLOs, including disciplinary actions such as fines, suspension, or revocation of licensure. These penalties underscore the critical nature of adherence to regulatory standards and the commitment of regulatory bodies to enforce these standards rigorously.

Moreover, the inclusion of the NMLS unique identifier in advertisements acts as a hallmark of professionalism and compliance, distinguishing compliant MLOs from those who may seek to evade oversight or engage in unscrupulous practices. It signals to consumers and industry peers alike that an MLO is committed to upholding the highest standards of ethical conduct and regulatory compliance.

The requirement to include the NMLS unique identifier in advertisements is a cornerstone of regulatory compliance for mortgage loan originators. It plays a pivotal role in safeguarding consumer interests, enhancing the transparency of the mortgage lending industry, and promoting an environment of trust and accountability. Compliance with this requirement is not only a legal obligation but also a critical component of professional integrity and reputation management in the mortgage industry.

Chapter 3: General Mortgage Knowledge

Qualified vs. Non-qualified Mortgage Programs

Qualified Mortgages and ATR Compliance

Qualified Mortgages (QMs) represent a significant segment of the mortgage industry, designed to provide safer and more stable loan products for consumers. The concept of Qualified Mortgages was introduced as part of the Dodd-Frank Wall Street Reform and Consumer Protection Act, aiming to protect borrowers from predatory lending practices and prevent the types of mortgage crises seen in the past. A cornerstone of the QM criteria is the Ability-to-Repay (ATR) rule, which mandates lenders to make a reasonable and good faith determination of a borrower's capability to fulfill the terms of their loan.

Under the ATR rule, lenders are required to consider eight specific underwriting factors when assessing a borrower's repayment ability. These factors include current income or assets, employment status, the monthly payment on the covered transaction, the monthly payment on any simultaneous loans, the monthly payment for mortgage-related obligations, current debt obligations, the monthly debt-to-income ratio or residual income, and credit history. This comprehensive assessment ensures that borrowers are not approved for loans that they cannot afford over the long term.

The Debt-to-Income (DTI) ratio is capped at 43% for QM loans, meaning a borrower's total monthly debts, including the mortgage, should not exceed 43% of their monthly pre-tax income. This cap is designed to ensure that borrowers have sufficient income to cover their debts and living expenses, reducing the risk of default.

One of the defining features of Qualified Mortgages is the absence of risky loan features. QMs prohibit terms that can significantly increase financial risk for borrowers, such as negative amortization, interest-only payments, balloon payments, or loan terms exceeding 30 years. These features, common in many non-QM loans, can lead to unexpected increases in a borrower's monthly payments or leave them owing more than the original loan amount.

Qualified Mortgages also provide legal protections for lenders, known as safe harbor. For prime QMs where the borrower's DTI is within the 43% threshold, lenders are given a presumption of compliance with the ATR rule, offering greater legal security against claims that they failed to assess the borrower's ability to repay the loan. However, for higher-priced QM loans typically offered to borrowers with lower credit scores or other risk factors, this presumption is rebuttable, meaning the borrower can challenge the lender's determination under certain conditions.

The QM standards aim to strike a balance between protecting consumers and providing lenders with the framework to offer sustainable mortgage products. By adhering to these criteria, lenders help ensure that borrowers receive loans they can afford over the long term, reducing the likelihood of default and foreclosure. This approach not only benefits individual borrowers and lenders but also contributes to the stability of the broader housing market and financial system.

Conforming Loans: Fannie Mae and Freddie Mac

Conventional or conforming loans are those that adhere to the guidelines set forth by Fannie Mae and Freddie Mac, two government-sponsored enterprises (GSEs) that play a significant role in the U.S. housing finance system. These loans are termed "conforming" because they conform to the loan limits and other criteria established by Fannie Mae and Freddie Mac. The primary purpose of these guidelines is to facilitate a more stable and accessible secondary mortgage market.

The conforming loan limits are adjusted annually based on the Federal Housing Finance Agency's (FHFA) house price index. For most counties in the United States, the baseline conforming loan limit for a single-family home in 2023 is set at $726,200. However, in high-cost areas, where real estate prices significantly exceed the national average, the loan limits can be higher. For instance, in certain high-cost counties, the limit for a single-family home can go up to $1,089,300. These elevated limits are designed to provide borrowers in expensive housing markets with access to affordable financing options.

Eligibility for a loan to be purchased by Fannie Mae or Freddie Mac requires adherence to their underwriting guidelines, which include borrower credit scores, debt-to-income ratios (DTI), loan-to-value ratios (LTV), and documentation of income and assets. Typically, Fannie Mae and Freddie Mac require a minimum credit score of 620 for a conventional loan, though higher scores may be necessary to secure the best interest rates and loan terms.

The DTI ratio, which compares a borrower's total monthly debt payments to their monthly gross income, is another critical factor in determining eligibility. Fannie Mae and Freddie Mac generally prefer a DTI ratio of no more than 45%, although cases with strong compensating factors may be considered with a DTI as high as 50%. This requirement ensures that borrowers are not over-leveraged and are more likely to manage their mortgage payments effectively.

For LTV, the maximum limit for a primary residence under a conforming loan is typically 97%, meaning borrowers can finance up to 97% of their home's value and need to provide a minimum down payment of 3%. This high LTV ratio is contingent upon the borrower meeting all other credit qualifications and, in many cases, completing a homeowner education course if they are a first-time homebuyer.

Stricter credit standards and borrower requirements for conventional loans are in place to mitigate the risk of default. By ensuring that borrowers have a strong credit history, a manageable level of debt compared to their income, and sufficient resources for a down payment, Fannie Mae and Freddie Mac can maintain the quality of the loans they purchase. This, in turn, supports the stability of the housing market and the broader financial system.

In addition to these criteria, borrowers seeking a conforming loan must also provide comprehensive documentation of their income and assets. This documentation can include W-2 forms, tax returns, pay stubs, and bank statements, which are used to verify the borrower's financial situation and ensure they have the capacity to repay the loan. The thorough vetting process for conforming loans underscores the importance of financial stability and responsibility in the homebuying process.

Government-Backed Loans: FHA, VA, USDA

Government-backed loans, such as those provided by the Federal Housing Administration (FHA), the U.S. Department of Veterans Affairs (VA), and the U.S. Department of Agriculture (USDA), play a pivotal role in the mortgage landscape by offering unique benefits tailored to specific groups of borrowers. These loans are designed to promote homeownership among those who might not qualify for conventional mortgages due to financial constraints or other factors.

The FHA loan program is renowned for its lower down payment requirements, typically as low as 3.5% of the purchase price. This feature makes it an attractive option for first-time homebuyers or those with limited savings. FHA loans are insured by the Federal Housing Administration, which protects lenders against defaults, thereby encouraging them to offer favorable loan terms. Borrowers are required to pay mortgage insurance premiums (MIP), which consist of an upfront fee and an annual fee, regardless of the down payment amount. This insurance is a critical component of the FHA program, as it reduces the risk to lenders.

VA loans, on the other hand, cater to veterans, active-duty service members, and certain members of the National Guard and Reserves. One of the most significant benefits of VA loans is the possibility of 0% down payment, making homeownership accessible without the need for substantial upfront capital. Additionally, VA loans do not require private mortgage insurance

(PMI), which can lead to considerable savings over the life of the loan. Instead, a one-time funding fee is charged at closing, which can be financed into the loan amount. The VA guarantees a portion of the loan, providing lenders with an added layer of security.

USDA loans target borrowers looking to purchase homes in rural and some suburban areas, aiming to boost economic development in less densely populated regions. These loans offer 100% financing, meaning no down payment is required, which significantly lowers the barrier to homeownership. To qualify, applicants must meet certain income limits, which vary by region and are designed to ensure that the program serves those with moderate to low incomes. USDA loans also come with a guarantee fee, similar to the VA's funding fee, which includes both an upfront and an annual charge.

Each of these government-backed loan programs has specific eligibility requirements. For FHA loans, borrowers must have a credit score of at least 580 to qualify for the 3.5% down payment option, though those with scores as low as 500 may still be eligible with a 10% down payment. VA loans require a suitable credit score, determined by the lender, and a Certificate of Eligibility (COE) to prove military service. USDA loans necessitate that the property be located in an eligible area and that the household income does not exceed the set limits.

The underwriting process for these loans also considers factors such as debt-to-income (DTI) ratios, with FHA and USDA programs generally allowing higher DTI ratios than conventional loans, thereby accommodating a broader range of financial situations. VA loans are particularly flexible, with no fixed DTI limit, instead focusing on the overall financial picture of the borrower.

Government-backed loans provide significant benefits for qualified borrowers, such as reduced down payment requirements, the absence of private mortgage insurance (PMI), and adaptable underwriting criteria. These programs play a crucial role in enhancing homeownership opportunities for veterans, families with low to moderate incomes, and first-time homebuyers, thereby fostering diversity and inclusivity within the housing market.

Nonconforming and Nontraditional Mortgages

Nonconforming loans, often referred to as **jumbo loans**, are mortgage loans that exceed the conforming loan limits set by the Federal Housing Finance Agency (FHFA). Unlike conventional loans that adhere to the purchasing criteria of Fannie Mae and Freddie Mac, jumbo loans are not eligible for purchase by these government-sponsored enterprises (GSEs). As a result, they typically carry higher interest rates to compensate for the increased risk lenders assume by extending these larger amounts of credit. Borrowers seeking jumbo loans must meet stringent credit requirements, including higher credit scores, lower debt-to-income ratios, and significant cash reserves.

Alt-A mortgages represent a category of home loans that fall between prime and subprime loans in terms of risk. These loans are often issued to borrowers with good credit scores but with other factors that increase the loan's risk, such as limited documentation of income or assets. Alt-A loans have historically been associated with higher interest rates than prime loans to compensate for the elevated risk. However, they also carry a higher risk of default than prime loans, as the less stringent documentation requirements can mask the borrower's true financial situation.

Subprime mortgages are designed for borrowers with poor credit histories who are considered a higher risk by lenders. These loans typically come with higher interest rates and fees to offset the increased risk of default. Subprime loans can be a pathway to homeownership for individuals who might not qualify for conventional mortgages, but they also carry significant risks, including higher costs and the potential for financial strain due to the elevated interest rates.

The **Ability-to-Repay (ATR) rule** is a key consideration in the issuance of non-qualified mortgages. This rule requires lenders to make a reasonable and good faith determination that the borrower has the ability to repay their loan. For non-qualified mortgages, certain exemptions to the ATR rule apply, allowing for more flexibility in loan terms and underwriting criteria. However, these exemptions also introduce additional risks, as they permit the issuance of loans without full verification of the borrower's ability to repay, potentially leading to higher default rates.

Nontraditional mortgage products, including jumbo, Alt-A, and subprime loans, present unique risks and considerations for both borrowers and lenders. For borrowers, the higher interest rates and less stringent documentation requirements can offer an opportunity for homeownership but also carry the risk of financial overextension and default. Lenders, on the other hand, face increased risk due to the higher loan amounts, elevated default rates, and regulatory scrutiny associated with these products.

In evaluating nontraditional mortgage products, it is crucial for both borrowers and lenders to carefully assess the risks and benefits. Borrowers should consider their long-term financial stability and the potential for changes in their income or property values that could affect their ability to repay the loan. Lenders must diligently evaluate the borrower's creditworthiness and the adequacy of loan terms to mitigate the risk of default. By understanding the complexities and risks associated with nonconforming, jumbo, Alt-A, and subprime mortgages, stakeholders can make informed decisions that align with their financial goals and risk tolerance.

Mortgage Loan Products

Fixed-Rate Mortgages Explained

Fixed-rate mortgages stand as a cornerstone of the mortgage industry, offering borrowers a stable and predictable financing option for home purchases. This type of mortgage locks in an interest rate that remains constant over the life of the loan, ensuring that the borrower's monthly principal and interest payments do not change from the first payment to the last. The consistency of the interest rate and monthly payments is particularly advantageous for individuals and families seeking financial stability and long-term budgeting predictability.

The terms for fixed-rate mortgages typically span 15, 20, or 30 years, with the 30-year fixed-rate mortgage being the most popular choice among homebuyers in the United States. The choice of term impacts the monthly payment amount and the total interest paid over the life of the loan. A 15-year term, for example, offers the benefit of paying off the mortgage in a shorter timeframe and accruing less interest, resulting in significant long-term savings. However, this comes at the cost of higher monthly payments. Conversely, a 30-year term lowers the monthly payment by spreading it out over a longer period, but the borrower will pay more in interest.

The interest rate on a fixed-rate mortgage is determined at the outset based on prevailing market conditions and the borrower's creditworthiness, among other factors. Once set, this rate does not fluctuate with market conditions, protecting borrowers from rising interest rates over the term of their loan. This predictability facilitates easier personal financial planning and budgeting, as borrowers know exactly what their mortgage payments will be for the duration of the loan.

Fixed-rate mortgages are particularly suitable for borrowers who plan on staying in their homes for an extended period. The stability of a fixed interest rate means that homeowners are not subjected to the risk of rising interest rates, which can significantly increase the cost of a mortgage. For those with a fixed or steadily increasing income, locking in a fixed rate can safeguard against the uncertainty of future interest rate environments and provide peace of mind.

Moreover, fixed-rate mortgages simplify the comparison of loan offers from different lenders, as the key variables are the interest rate and the loan term. Borrowers can easily evaluate the long-term financial implications of different interest rates and terms, making it easier to select a mortgage that best fits their financial goals and circumstances.

Fixed-rate mortgages provide a combination of predictability, stability, and simplicity, making them a favored option for numerous homebuyers. By securing a fixed interest rate for the life of the loan, borrowers can protect themselves against fluctuations in the interest rate market, ensuring that their home remains an affordable and stable investment. Whether opting for a shorter-term loan to build equity quickly and save on interest, or a longer-term loan to reduce monthly payments, fixed-rate mortgages provide a reliable financing option for achieving homeownership goals.

Adjustable-Rate Mortgages Explained

Adjustable-rate mortgages (ARMs) present a dynamic financing option in the mortgage landscape, characterized by interest rates that can fluctuate over the loan's term, as opposed to the fixed interest rate applied throughout the duration of a fixed-rate mortgage. This variability in interest rates is primarily influenced by broader economic trends and changes in market conditions, making ARMs inherently more complex and necessitating a thorough understanding of their components and potential impacts on borrowers' financial obligations.

The initial fixed period of an ARM is a critical feature, offering borrowers a lower interest rate that remains constant for a predetermined time frame at the start of the loan term. This period typically ranges from one to ten years, depending on the specific product. The appeal of this initial phase lies in the reduced interest rate compared to fixed-rate mortgages, potentially offering significant savings in the early years of the mortgage. However, once this period concludes, the interest rate adjusts at regular intervals, which can lead to higher or lower monthly payments for the remainder of the loan term.

Interest rate adjustments in ARMs are governed by two key components: the index and the margin. The index is a benchmark interest rate reflecting general market conditions, such as the London Interbank Offered Rate (LIBOR) or the Secured Overnight Financing Rate (SOFR), which lenders use to determine the ARM's interest rate adjustments. The margin, on the other hand, is a fixed percentage point that lenders add to the index to set the ARM's interest rate after the initial fixed period. The combination of the index and the margin determines the adjusted interest rate at each adjustment period.

Rate caps play a pivotal role in ARMs, providing a safeguard for borrowers by limiting the degree to which the interest rate can change during adjustment periods and over the life of the loan. There are typically three types of caps: initial adjustment cap, which limits the interest rate increase at the first adjustment; periodic adjustment cap, which limits the interest rate change from one adjustment period to the next; and the lifetime cap, which sets a maximum limit on interest rate increases over the loan's term. These caps are essential for borrowers to understand, as they directly impact the potential fluctuation in monthly payments and the overall cost of borrowing.

The risks and rewards associated with ARMs are closely tied to the fluctuation of interest rates and the borrower's financial situation. The primary advantage lies in the potential for lower initial payments, which can be particularly appealing for borrowers expecting an increase in income or those planning to sell or refinance their home before the end of the initial fixed period. However, the uncertainty of future rate adjustments introduces a significant risk, as rising interest rates can lead to increased monthly payments, potentially straining the borrower's finances. This unpredictability necessitates careful consideration and planning, as well as a clear understanding of the loan's terms and conditions.

In evaluating whether an ARM is a suitable mortgage product, borrowers must consider their long-term financial goals, risk tolerance, and the potential for changes in interest rates over time. Understanding the structure and components of ARMs, including the initial fixed period, rate caps, index, and margin, is crucial for making informed decisions that align with one's financial objectives and circumstances.

Purchase Money Second Mortgages

Purchase money second mortgages serve as a strategic financing option for homebuyers looking to manage their initial investment and monthly expenses more effectively. These secondary loans are specifically designed to finance down payments or cover part of the purchase price of a property, thereby reducing the principal amount of the primary mortgage. This financial maneuver is particularly advantageous for buyers aiming to lower their loan-to-value (LTV) ratio to a level that circumvents the requirement for private mortgage insurance (PMI), a common additional cost for mortgages with less than 20% down payment.

The mechanics of a purchase money second mortgage involve taking out a second loan at the time of purchasing the property. This loan is subordinate to the primary mortgage, meaning in the event of a default, the primary mortgage is prioritized for repayment before any funds are allocated to the second mortgage. The interest rates on these second mortgages are typically higher than those of the primary mortgages due to the increased risk to lenders, and the terms can vary significantly based on the lender's policies and the borrower's creditworthiness.

One of the key benefits of utilizing a purchase money second mortgage is the potential to avoid PMI. PMI is designed to protect lenders from the increased risk associated with high LTV loans. By effectively lowering the LTV ratio through the combination of the first and second mortgages, borrowers can often bypass this requirement, resulting in significant savings over the life of the loan. For example, if a borrower purchases a home for $300,000 with a 10% down payment ($30,000) and secures a purchase money second mortgage for an additional 10%

($30,000), the primary mortgage would be based on an 80% LTV ratio ($240,000), thus avoiding PMI.

Furthermore, this financing strategy can provide buyers with more flexibility in managing their cash flow and investment in the property. By reducing the size of the primary mortgage, borrowers can achieve lower monthly payments, which may be more aligned with their financial goals and constraints. Additionally, the interest paid on both the first and second mortgages is typically tax-deductible, providing further financial benefit to the borrower.

However, it's crucial for potential borrowers to carefully consider the terms and conditions of both the primary and secondary loans. The combined monthly payments of both mortgages should be sustainable over the long term, taking into account the borrower's income stability and other financial obligations. Borrowers should also be aware of any prepayment penalties, balloon payments, or other terms that could affect their ability to manage or refinance the loans in the future.

In conclusion, purchase money second mortgages offer a viable option for homebuyers looking to minimize their down payment, avoid PMI, and manage their monthly mortgage expenses more effectively. By understanding the structure, benefits, and considerations associated with these loans, borrowers can make informed decisions that align with their financial objectives and housing needs.

Balloon Mortgages: Risks and Refinancing

Balloon mortgages are a unique financing option that offers lower initial payments followed by a large, lump-sum payment at the end of the loan term. This structure allows borrowers to benefit from reduced payment amounts during the majority of the loan's lifespan, typically ranging from 5 to 7 years, before the balloon payment is due. The final balloon payment covers the remaining principal balance and can be significantly larger than the preceding installment payments.

The primary appeal of balloon mortgages lies in the lower monthly payments during the initial period. This can be particularly advantageous for borrowers expecting to increase their income over time, sell the property before the balloon payment is due, or refinance into a new loan with more favorable terms. However, the risks associated with this type of mortgage cannot be overstated. If borrowers are unable to make the balloon payment when it comes due, they face the risk of defaulting on the loan, which could lead to foreclosure. Additionally, if property values decline or if borrowers' financial situations worsen, refinancing to cover the balloon payment may not be an option.

Refinancing options are a critical consideration for anyone with a balloon mortgage. Ideally, borrowers will have built enough equity in their home and improved their financial standing to qualify for a refinance into a traditional fixed-rate or adjustable-rate mortgage (ARM) by the time the balloon payment is due. This strategy requires careful planning and awareness of market conditions, as interest rates at the time of refinancing could significantly impact the affordability of new loan terms.

It's essential for borrowers to understand the terms of their balloon mortgage, including any potential penalties for early payoff and the process for refinancing with their lender. Lenders may offer a conversion feature that allows the balloon mortgage to automatically convert into a new loan with a longer term, though this is not guaranteed and may come with additional costs.

Given the risks associated with the inability to pay the balloon payment, borrowers must have a clear exit strategy before entering into a balloon mortgage. This could include plans for selling the property, refinancing, or making financial adjustments to afford the balloon payment. Financial advisors often recommend that borrowers set aside additional savings or make extra payments towards the principal balance when possible to reduce the size of the balloon payment and mitigate the risk of default.

While balloon mortgages can provide temporary financial relief through reduced monthly payments, they carry considerable risks that necessitate thorough consideration and planning. Borrowers must assess their long-term financial stability, the likelihood of refinancing, and the prevailing conditions in the real estate market to ensure they can handle the balloon payment when it becomes due.

Reverse Mortgages: Eligibility and Risks

Reverse mortgages represent a distinctive financial product designed for homeowners aged 62 and over, offering them the opportunity to convert part of their home equity into cash income without the obligation to make monthly mortgage payments. This financial arrangement allows seniors to tap into the equity they have built up in their homes, providing a source of income while enabling them to remain in their homes during their retirement years.

Eligibility for a reverse mortgage requires that at least one homeowner is 62 years of age or older. The property in question must be the primary residence, meaning the homeowner must live in the home for the majority of the year. Additionally, the property must meet all FHA property standards and flood requirements. The homeowner is also required to have a considerable amount of equity in the home, typically at least 50%, and the property must be either fully paid off or have a low balance that can be paid off at closing with proceeds from the reverse mortgage.

The process of converting equity into income can be structured in several ways, including lump sum payments, monthly payments, a line of credit, or a combination of these options. The amount of money a homeowner can borrow depends on several factors, including the age of the youngest borrower or eligible non-borrowing spouse, current interest rates, the appraised value of the home, and the initial mortgage insurance premium.

One of the most critical aspects of reverse mortgages is that the borrower is not required to pay back the loan until the home is sold, the borrower moves out, or the borrower passes away. However, borrowers are still responsible for maintaining the property, paying property taxes, homeowner's insurance, and any homeowners association (HOA) fees.

Despite the benefits, reverse mortgages come with several associated fees and risks. These include an origination fee, upfront mortgage insurance premium (MIP), ongoing MIP charges, and servicing fees. The interest on a reverse mortgage accumulates over time, increasing the loan balance, while the home equity decreases. This aspect is crucial for heirs to understand, as it affects the amount of equity that can be passed on.

Furthermore, if the homeowner fails to meet the loan obligations, such as paying property taxes and insurance, the loan may become due and payable, potentially leading to foreclosure. Therefore, potential borrowers must carefully consider their ability to meet these ongoing requirements before proceeding with a reverse mortgage.

Reverse mortgages can offer financial relief and greater flexibility in retirement for eligible homeowners. However, it's essential for individuals to thoroughly understand the terms, conditions, and responsibilities associated with this type of loan, as well as to consider their long-term financial planning and any potential impact on their estate.

Home Equity Line of Credit (HELOC)

A Home Equity Line of Credit (HELOC) is a revolving credit line that allows homeowners to borrow against the equity in their home. Unlike a traditional home equity loan, which provides a lump sum upfront, a HELOC offers a credit limit that borrowers can draw from as needed, similar to a credit card but with the home serving as collateral. The amount available to borrow is based on the current value of the home minus any outstanding mortgage balance. This financial product is particularly attractive due to its flexibility and potential tax benefits, as the interest may be tax-deductible if used for home improvement or other qualifying expenses.

Variable Interest Rates are a hallmark of HELOCs. The interest rate on a HELOC is typically tied to a publicly available index, such as the prime rate, plus a margin determined by the lender. This means the interest rate can fluctuate over the life of the line of credit, affecting the monthly payment amounts. Borrowers should be aware of any caps on how high or low the interest rate can go and any periods of fixed interest rates that some lenders may offer.

Draw Periods in a HELOC typically last 5 to 10 years, during which the borrower can access the funds up to the credit limit, repay them, and borrow again. After the draw period ends, the repayment period begins, usually lasting 10 to 20 years, during which withdrawals are no longer allowed, and the outstanding balance must be repaid. It's crucial for borrowers to understand the terms of their HELOC, as some may require a balloon payment at the end of the draw period, where the entire remaining balance is due all at once.

Common uses of HELOC funds include **home improvement projects**, which can increase the value of the home and potentially provide a return on investment when the home is sold. Other uses include consolidating high-interest debt, financing major expenses such as education or medical bills, and serving as an emergency fund. However, borrowers should exercise caution and consider their ability to repay the loan, as defaulting on a HELOC could result in foreclosure.

When considering a HELOC, it's essential to compare offers from multiple lenders, as terms, interest rates, fees, and repayment options can vary significantly. Borrowers should also assess their financial situation and goals, ensuring that a HELOC is the most appropriate and cost-effective option for their needs. Additionally, maintaining open communication with the lender throughout the life of the HELOC can help manage any financial changes that may affect the loan.

A HELOC provides homeowners with a flexible and potentially tax-advantaged method to access the equity in their property. Recognizing the essential characteristics, such as variable interest rates and draw periods, along with utilizing the funds for strategic purposes like home improvement, enables borrowers to effectively use a HELOC to achieve their financial objectives while managing the associated risks of variable debt products.

Construction Mortgages Explained

Construction mortgages, also known as construction loans, serve as a vital financial tool for individuals or developers looking to build a home or undertake significant renovations. Unlike traditional mortgages, construction mortgages are designed to finance the construction phase of a home, which typically involves a series of payments that are disbursed to the builder or contractor as various stages of the construction process are completed. These loans are characterized by their short-term nature, usually ranging from six months to one year, and are not meant to provide permanent financing for the borrower. Instead, they are intended to bridge the gap between the commencement of construction and the completion of the home, at which point a more traditional, long-term mortgage is used to pay off the construction loan.

One of the unique features of construction mortgages is the interest-only payment structure during the construction period. Borrowers are generally required to make interest-only payments on the funds that have been disbursed up to that point. This payment structure is particularly beneficial for borrowers during the construction phase, as it minimizes their financial burden during a period when they may also need to cover the costs of temporary housing or storage. The interest rate on a construction mortgage is typically variable, pegged to a standard rate such as the prime rate plus a margin. This means that the interest rate, and thus the interest payments, can fluctuate during the construction period based on prevailing economic conditions.

The disbursement of funds from a construction mortgage is closely tied to the construction schedule and progress. Lenders typically require an inspection or appraisal to verify that a specified stage of construction has been completed before releasing the next draw of funds. This draw schedule is established at the onset of the loan and is designed to ensure that the project progresses as planned and that funds are used appropriately.

Upon completion of the construction, the borrower must transition from the construction mortgage to permanent financing. This transition can occur in one of two ways: a one-time close or a two-time close. In a one-time close, also known as a "construction-to-permanent" loan, the construction loan is converted into a standard mortgage once construction is complete. This approach offers the advantage of locking in the interest rate for the permanent loan at the time of closing the construction loan, providing borrowers with rate security. However, it may come with higher initial costs or stricter qualification criteria due to the long-term commitment from the lender.

In contrast, a two-time close involves obtaining a separate construction loan for the building phase and then refinancing with a new loan for permanent financing once construction is completed. This method provides flexibility for borrowers to shop for the best mortgage terms and rates available post-construction but involves two sets of closing costs and the risk of interest rate fluctuations.

For borrowers, understanding the intricacies of construction mortgages is crucial. They must be prepared for the potential financial implications of delays in construction, changes in interest rates, and the requirements for transitioning to permanent financing. Additionally, borrowers should meticulously plan their construction budget and timeline, considering the draw schedule and the need for inspections or appraisals to facilitate fund releases. Engaging with a lender experienced in construction financing and having a clear agreement with the builder or contractor can help ensure a smooth process from the planning stage through to the completion of the home and the transition to long-term financing.

Interest-Only Mortgages Explained

Interest-only mortgages present a unique financial structure within the realm of mortgage loan products, characterized by an initial period during which the borrower is required to make payments solely on the interest accrued by the loan, without reducing the principal balance. This period typically spans several years at the beginning of the loan term. Following this phase, the mortgage transitions into a standard amortizing loan, where payments cover both interest and principal, significantly increasing the monthly financial commitment for the borrower.

The appeal of an interest-only mortgage lies in the substantially lower monthly payments during the interest-only period. This feature can be particularly attractive to borrowers with fluctuating income, such as those who receive significant portions of their income from bonuses, commissions, or seasonal work. It allows for greater cash flow flexibility during the initial years of homeownership, potentially enabling borrowers to allocate funds towards investments, debt reduction, or savings that might yield a higher return than the immediate reduction of mortgage principal.

However, the structure of interest-only mortgages introduces several risks and considerations that must be meticulously evaluated. Firstly, the lack of principal reduction during the initial phase of the loan means that the borrower does not build equity in the property through their monthly payments, unless there is an appreciation in the property's market value. This situation can become particularly precarious in a declining market, where the borrower may find themselves owing more on the mortgage than the home is worth, a condition known as being "underwater" on a mortgage.

Furthermore, once the interest-only period concludes, borrowers face a significant increase in monthly payments. This adjustment can lead to financial strain for those who have not planned adequately for the transition. The recalculated payments are higher than they would have been from the start of a traditional amortizing mortgage because they are spread over a shorter remaining term. For example, if a borrower has a 30-year mortgage with a 10-year interest-only period, the principal must be repaid over the remaining 20 years, leading to higher monthly payments than if the loan had been amortizing from the beginning.

The long-term costs associated with interest-only mortgages can also be higher compared to traditional mortgages. Over the life of the loan, borrowers pay more in interest charges because they delay principal repayment. This aspect means that for each dollar borrowed, the total interest paid over the life of an interest-only mortgage can significantly exceed that of a traditional mortgage, where principal reduction begins immediately.

Borrowers considering an interest-only mortgage must also be mindful of the qualification criteria, which can be more stringent due to the increased risk these loans pose to lenders. Lenders may require higher credit scores, larger down payments, and more substantial proof of income and assets to ensure that borrowers can handle the higher payments once the interest-only period ends.

In assessing the suitability of an interest-only mortgage, potential borrowers should conduct a thorough analysis of their long-term financial strategy, considering not only the initial period of lower payments but also the implications of higher future payments and the overall cost of the loan. It is crucial to have a robust plan for managing the transition to amortizing payments, including considerations for refinancing options, potential changes in income, and market conditions that could affect property value and equity accumulation.

Interest-only mortgages, while offering an attractive pathway to homeownership with lower initial payments, demand careful consideration and planning due to the inherent risks and long-term financial implications. Borrowers must weigh these factors diligently, aligning their mortgage choice with their financial goals, risk tolerance, and future income prospects to ensure a sustainable and prudent approach to property financing.

Mortgage Industry Terminology

Loan Terms and Concepts Explained

Subordinate loans, often referred to as second mortgages, are loans where the lien position is secondary to the primary mortgage. In the event of a foreclosure, the primary mortgage is paid off first, and any remaining funds then go towards the subordinate loan. This positioning impacts the risk assessment and interest rates of these loans, as they are considered higher risk than primary mortgages.

Escrow accounts are pivotal in managing the ongoing expenses associated with a property, such as taxes and insurance. These accounts collect a portion of these expenses with each mortgage payment, ensuring that funds are available when these payments are due. This mitigates the risk of tax liens against the property and ensures that the property remains insured.

A lien is a legal right or claim against a property by a creditor. Liens must be paid off for a property to be sold or refinanced. The priority of liens is crucial in the event of a sale or foreclosure, as it determines the order in which creditors are paid. Mortgage liens have priority based on their recording date, with earlier liens receiving payment before later ones.

Tolerances in the mortgage process refer to the allowable variations between estimated and actual closing costs. The Real Estate Settlement Procedures Act (RESPA) specifies tolerances for certain fees, limiting how much they can increase between the Loan Estimate and the Closing Disclosure. Zero tolerance fees, such as origination charges, cannot increase, while others have a 10% cumulative tolerance. This protects borrowers from significant unexpected increases in closing costs.

Rate lock agreements allow borrowers to lock in an interest rate for a specified period, protecting them from rate increases during the mortgage process. This agreement provides financial predictability for the borrower but may come with a fee, especially for longer lock periods. If rates decrease, the borrower may not benefit from the lower rate unless they have a float-down provision in their rate lock agreement.

Table funding is a process where a loan is funded at closing by a third party, typically a lender, rather than the originator of the loan. This allows for quicker closings, as the funds are immediately available. In table funding, the originator sells the loan to the funding lender at the closing table, and the transaction is recorded in the name of the lender. This practice is common in states where immediate funding is required by law and facilitates smoother, more efficient closings for all parties involved.

Disclosure Terms in Mortgage Lending

Yield Spread Premiums (YSP) serve as a form of compensation for mortgage brokers, originating from the difference between the interest rate a borrower is charged and the rate for which the borrower qualifies. Essentially, if a broker can secure a loan for a borrower at an interest rate higher than the wholesale rate, the lender may pay the broker this difference as a YSP. This practice incentivizes brokers to find lenders willing to fund mortgages, though it's crucial for brokers to disclose YSPs to borrowers, ensuring transparency and compliance with federal regulations.

Federal mortgage loans, such as those backed by the Federal Housing Administration (FHA), Veterans Affairs (VA), or the United States Department of Agriculture (USDA), come with specific characteristics. These loans are designed to lower the entry barrier for homeownership, offering benefits like lower down payments, more lenient credit requirements, and government insurance to protect lenders against default. However, they also come with unique requirements for approval and servicing, including mandatory mortgage insurance premiums for certain loan types.

Servicing transfers between lenders or servicing companies can occur during the life of a mortgage loan. Federal law requires that borrowers be notified in writing both before and after a servicing transfer. This notification must include information such as the new servicer's name and contact details, the date the new servicer will begin accepting payments, and any changes to the terms or conditions of the mortgage. These regulations ensure that borrowers are well-informed of who is managing their loan and where their mortgage payments should be sent, minimizing confusion and potential payment errors.

Lender credits are another critical term in mortgage lending, acting as a mechanism to reduce closing costs for the borrower. In exchange for agreeing to a higher interest rate on their loan, a borrower can receive credits from the lender to cover part or all of the upfront costs associated with securing a mortgage. This can significantly lower the amount of cash a borrower needs to bring to closing. However, it's important for borrowers to understand that while lender credits can reduce initial expenses, the higher interest rate over the life of the loan may result in paying more in interest over time.

Financial Terms Explained

Discount Points are a form of prepaid interest that borrowers can purchase to lower the interest rate on their loans. One discount point is equivalent to 1% of the loan amount and typically reduces the interest rate by 0.25%, although this reduction can vary by lender and market conditions. The decision to buy discount points should be based on a break-even analysis, calculating how long it will take for the monthly savings from the lower interest rate to exceed the upfront cost of the points. The formula for this calculation is:

$$\text{Break-even point (in months)} = \frac{\text{Total cost of discount points}}{\text{Monthly savings from reduced interest rate}}$$

2-1 Buy-Down is a financing technique where the interest rate on the mortgage is reduced by 2% for the first year and 1% for the second year. From the third year onwards, the interest rate reverts to the standard rate. This arrangement is often funded by the seller as an incentive to the buyer, effectively lowering the borrower's initial monthly payments, which gradually increase to the normal rate after two years. This strategy can be particularly appealing in a buyer's market or when the seller is eager to expedite the sale.

Loan-to-Value (LTV) Ratio is a critical metric used by lenders to assess the risk of a mortgage loan. It is calculated by dividing the loan amount by the appraised value of the property:

$$\text{LTV Ratio} = \frac{\text{Loan Amount}}{\text{Appraised Property Value}}$$

Lenders typically require a maximum LTV ratio of 80%, meaning the borrower must make a down payment of at least 20% of the property's value. Higher LTV ratios may require the purchase of Private Mortgage Insurance (PMI) to mitigate the lender's risk.

Accrued Interest refers to the interest that accumulates on a loan between payment periods. For mortgages, interest is usually calculated monthly, based on the principal balance of the loan. The formula for calculating accrued interest is:

$$\text{Accrued Interest} = \frac{\text{Annual Interest Rate}}{12} \times \text{Principal Balance}$$

Finance Charges encompass all costs associated with obtaining a mortgage, including interest, service charges, credit report fees, and insurance premiums. The Total Finance Charge over the life of the loan reflects the total cost of borrowing and is crucial for comparing the cost-effectiveness of different mortgage offers.

Daily Simple Interest calculations are used for some types of loans, where interest accrues daily rather than monthly. The formula for daily simple interest is:

$$\text{Daily Interest} = \frac{\text{Annual Interest Rate}}{365} \times \text{Principal Balance}$$

This method means that the actual amount of interest accrued can vary depending on the number of days in each month and whether it's a leap year, affecting the total interest paid over the life of the loan.

Understanding these financial terms and calculations is essential for mortgage professionals and borrowers alike, enabling informed decision-making and effective financial planning in the mortgage process.

General Terms: Subordination to APR

Subordination agreements are pivotal in the realm of mortgage lending, establishing a hierarchy among creditors in the event of a borrower's default or property sale. These agreements are particularly relevant when a homeowner seeks to refinance the first mortgage without paying off an existing second mortgage or home equity line of credit. The subordination agreement ensures that the new first mortgage takes precedence over existing secondary liens, thereby maintaining the priority order of claims. This arrangement is crucial for lenders to manage risk, as it affects the likelihood of recouping their investment in foreclosure scenarios.

Property conveyance refers to the legal process of transferring ownership of real property from one party to another. This process is formalized through a deed, a legal document that outlines the specifics of the property transfer, including the identities of the old and new owners, a detailed description of the property, and any conditions or warranties. The conveyance process is integral to the mortgage industry, as it ensures the legal transfer of property rights, which is essential for securing the collateral that underpins mortgage lending.

The primary and secondary mortgage markets play distinct yet interconnected roles in the financing of real estate. The primary market is where borrowers and mortgage originators come together to negotiate terms and create initial mortgage loans. This direct interaction facilitates the origination of loans tailored to the financial situations of borrowers. Conversely, the secondary market involves the sale and purchase of existing mortgages or mortgage-backed securities. This market provides liquidity to the primary market lenders, enabling them to offer more loans by selling existing mortgages to investors, including government-sponsored enterprises like Fannie Mae and Freddie Mac.

Third-party providers in the mortgage industry offer a range of services that support the origination, processing, and closing of mortgage loans. These entities include appraisal companies, title insurance firms, credit reporting agencies, and legal services. Their roles are critical in providing the necessary due diligence, valuation, and legal compliance required for mortgage transactions. By ensuring that all aspects of the loan are accurately assessed and legally sound, third-party providers help mitigate the risk for lenders and borrowers alike.

Assumable loans are a unique type of mortgage that allows a new buyer to take over the seller's existing mortgage under its current terms, rather than obtaining a new mortgage. This feature can be particularly attractive in a rising interest rate environment, as it enables the buyer to benefit from the seller's lower interest rate. However, not all loans are assumable, and lenders typically require the new borrower to qualify under their credit criteria before allowing the assumption to proceed.

The Annual Percentage Rate (APR) represents the total cost of borrowing on a yearly basis, expressed as a percentage. Unlike the nominal interest rate, the APR includes not only the interest expense but also any additional fees or costs associated with securing the mortgage, such as origination fees, points, and certain closing costs. The APR is a critical measure for borrowers to consider, as it provides a more comprehensive view of the loan's cost compared to the interest rate alone. By evaluating the APR, borrowers can make more informed comparisons between different loan offers, ensuring they choose the most cost-effective financing option for their needs.

Each of these terms plays a vital role in the landscape of mortgage lending, affecting the rights, responsibilities, and financial outcomes for all parties involved. From the legal frameworks that govern property ownership and creditor priorities to the mechanisms that ensure liquidity and risk management in the mortgage market, understanding these concepts is essential for professionals navigating the complex terrain of real estate finance.

Chapter 4: Mortgage Loan Origination

Loan Inquiry and Application Process

Loan Inquiry Disclosures

During the loan inquiry process, potential borrowers are entitled to receive specific disclosures that are mandated by federal law to ensure transparency and fairness in the mortgage lending process. These disclosures are designed to provide borrowers with the critical information needed to make informed decisions about their mortgage options. Understanding these disclosures, including the timing for the Loan Estimate, servicing disclosure, and homeownership counseling resources, is crucial for both mortgage professionals and applicants.

The Loan Estimate is a pivotal document in the mortgage application process. It must be provided to the borrower no later than three business days after the receipt of a complete mortgage loan application. This document outlines the estimated interest rate, monthly payment, and total closing costs for the loan. It also details loan terms, projected payments over the life of the loan, and the services for which the borrower can and cannot shop in relation to closing costs. The Loan Estimate serves as a critical tool for borrowers to compare costs and features of different loans and lenders, facilitating a more transparent and competitive lending environment.

Servicing disclosures are also a required part of the loan inquiry process. These disclosures inform the borrower whether the lender intends to service the loan or transfer it to another company for servicing. This disclosure must be provided to the borrower at the time of application or within three business days. Understanding who will service the loan is important for borrowers as it affects where and how they will make their mortgage payments and who they will communicate with should issues or questions arise regarding their loan.

Homeownership counseling resources must be made available to borrowers as part of the loan inquiry process, particularly for first-time homebuyers or those participating in certain types of loans, such as high-cost mortgages. Lenders are required to provide a list of HUD-approved housing counseling agencies. These agencies offer valuable information and assistance on home buying, fair lending, and foreclosure prevention. Providing access to homeownership counseling resources supports informed decision-making and promotes successful, sustainable homeownership.

It is essential for mortgage professionals to ensure that all required disclosures are provided accurately and timely, adhering to the regulations that govern the mortgage lending process. These disclosures not only fulfill legal requirements but also build trust with borrowers by fostering transparency and enabling them to make educated decisions regarding their mortgage options. The provision of these disclosures reflects the commitment of the mortgage industry to uphold ethical standards and protect consumers in the complex process of financing a home.

Borrower Application Process

The borrower application process is a critical phase in mortgage loan origination, requiring meticulous attention to detail and adherence to regulatory standards. Accepting applications involves collecting comprehensive personal and financial information from potential borrowers to assess their creditworthiness and eligibility for a mortgage loan. Mortgage Loan Originators (MLOs) must ensure that applications are filled out completely and accurately, verifying the information provided against documentation such as tax returns, pay stubs, and bank statements.

Offering and negotiating terms is another crucial aspect, where MLOs present loan options suitable to the borrower's financial situation and discuss the terms, including interest rates, repayment periods, and any other loan-specific conditions. It is imperative that MLOs communicate clearly and transparently, providing borrowers with all necessary information to make informed decisions. This stage often involves discussing various loan products and terms, allowing borrowers to compare options and choose the one that best fits their needs.

Managing sensitive borrower information is a responsibility that MLOs must handle with the utmost care. Privacy laws and regulations require that all personal and financial data be kept secure and confidential. MLOs must ensure that their data handling practices comply with the Gramm-Leach-Bliley Act (GLBA) and other applicable privacy regulations, safeguarding against unauthorized access or disclosure.

Permissible questions during the application process are governed by laws such as the Equal Credit Opportunity Act (ECOA) and the Fair Housing Act, which prohibit discrimination based on race, color, religion, national origin, sex, marital status, age, or dependency on public assistance. MLOs can ask questions related to financial stability, employment history, creditworthiness, and other relevant factors that affect the borrower's ability to repay the loan. However, questions that could be construed as discriminatory are strictly off-limits.

Gift donors often play a role in the mortgage process, providing funds to assist borrowers with down payments or closing costs. MLOs must document gift funds accurately, ensuring that the source of the funds is legitimate and that the gift does not need to be repaid. This documentation typically includes a gift letter from the donor, stating the relationship to the borrower, the amount of the gift, and the declaration that the funds are indeed a gift and not a loan. The donor may also need to provide proof of the ability to give the gift, such as bank statements or withdrawal documentation.

The borrower application process is a foundational component of mortgage loan origination, demanding precision, transparency, and adherence to legal and regulatory standards. MLOs play a pivotal role in guiding borrowers through this process, offering tailored loan options, managing sensitive information securely, and ensuring that all aspects of the application are compliant with federal and state laws.

Verification Steps for Loan Applications

The verification process in mortgage loan origination is a critical step to ensure the accuracy of the information provided by the borrower and to assess their financial stability and ability to repay the loan. This process involves several key components, including obtaining authorization forms, verifying the percentage of bank account assets attributable toward a loan application, and verifying employment for consistent income.

Firstly, obtaining borrower consent through authorization forms is paramount. These forms are legally required documents that grant the mortgage loan originator (MLO) permission to verify the borrower's information with third parties. The authorization must be explicit, detailing what information will be verified and with whom it will be shared. This step not only complies with privacy laws and regulations but also protects the lender by ensuring that the verification process is transparent and consented to by the borrower.

The verification of bank account assets plays a significant role in determining the borrower's financial health and liquidity. MLOs must ascertain what percentage of the borrower's assets are being allocated toward the loan application. This involves reviewing bank statements and other financial documents to ensure that the assets claimed on the application are present and accurately reflected. The MLO must pay close attention to recent large deposits or withdrawals, as these could indicate borrowed money being temporarily placed in the account to inflate the borrower's assets. A thorough analysis includes calculating the ratio of liquid assets to the loan amount, ensuring that the borrower has sufficient funds for the down payment, closing costs, and reserves as required by the lender's guidelines.

Verifying employment is another crucial step in the verification process. Consistent income is a key indicator of a borrower's ability to repay the loan. This verification is typically achieved through direct contact with the borrower's employer, reviewing recent pay stubs, and examining

W-2 forms or tax returns for self-employed individuals. The MLO must confirm the borrower's position, length of employment, salary, and the likelihood of continued employment. Special attention should be given to any gaps in employment or significant changes in income, as these could impact the borrower's financial stability.

In addition to these primary verification steps, the MLO may also need to verify other sources of income, such as bonuses, commissions, rental income, or income from investments. Each type of income may require different documents for verification, such as lease agreements for rental income or investment statements for dividend income. The key is to ensure that all income is verifiable, consistent, and sustainable over the long term to support the loan repayment.

Throughout the verification process, the MLO must adhere to strict ethical standards, ensuring that all information is obtained and handled with the utmost confidentiality and integrity. The goal is to build a complete and accurate picture of the borrower's financial situation, enabling informed decision-making regarding loan approval. This meticulous approach to verification not only protects the lender but also contributes to the overall stability of the mortgage lending system by ensuring that loans are granted to borrowers who are truly capable of repayment.

Suitability of Loan Products & Programs

Assessing borrower needs and matching them with suitable mortgage products and programs is a critical responsibility of Mortgage Loan Originators (MLOs). This process requires a deep understanding of the diverse range of mortgage options available and the ability to analyze the financial situation, goals, and preferences of each borrower. The ultimate objective is to ensure that the loan terms and program details are clearly reflected on the mortgage application, providing transparency and facilitating informed decision-making.

To effectively match borrowers with the most appropriate mortgage products, MLOs must first conduct a comprehensive assessment of the borrower's financial health. This includes evaluating their income stability, debt-to-income (DTI) ratio, credit history, and available assets for down payment and closing costs. Additionally, understanding the borrower's long-term financial goals and preferences, such as their comfort level with fluctuating payments or their plans for the property, is essential in identifying the most suitable loan options.

Once the borrower's needs and qualifications are clearly understood, MLOs can then navigate the complex landscape of mortgage products to find a match that aligns with the borrower's financial situation and objectives. This could range from fixed-rate mortgages for those seeking payment stability, adjustable-rate mortgages for those anticipating income growth or a short-term stay in the home, government-backed loans like FHA or VA for those needing lower down payments or with less-than-perfect credit, or jumbo loans for high-value properties.

The selection of a suitable mortgage product is only the beginning. MLOs must also ensure that the loan terms and program details are accurately and clearly reflected on the mortgage application. This includes the interest rate, loan term, repayment schedule, any special loan features (e.g., balloon payments, adjustable rates), and borrower responsibilities. Transparency in how these details are presented on the application not only aids in borrower understanding and satisfaction but also ensures compliance with lending regulations and standards.

Moreover, MLOs play a pivotal role in educating borrowers about the implications of different loan options. This involves explaining the mechanics of how interest rates affect monthly payments and the overall cost of the loan, the potential for payment changes over time with adjustable-rate mortgages, and the specifics of any government program requirements or benefits. By providing this education, MLOs empower borrowers to make choices that best suit their financial situation and goals.

The process of assessing borrower needs, matching them with suitable mortgage products, and clearly reflecting loan terms and program details on applications is a multifaceted responsibility that requires expertise, careful analysis, and clear communication. Through this process, MLOs can guide borrowers towards making informed decisions that align with their financial goals, ensuring a positive outcome for all parties involved in the mortgage transaction.

Accuracy and Tolerance in Service Charges

In the realm of mortgage loan origination, the accuracy of service charges and adherence to established tolerance levels are paramount. The Real Estate Settlement Procedures Act (RESPA) and the Truth in Lending Act (TILA) set forth rigorous requirements to ensure transparency and fairness in lending practices. These regulations categorize certain fees and charges into zero tolerance and 10% tolerance buckets, each with specific rules governing permissible variations between estimated and actual charges.

Zero tolerance charges are those fees over which lenders have direct control and are not permitted to increase from the initial Loan Estimate to the Closing Disclosure. These include the lender's origination fees, application fees, and underwriting fees. The rationale behind the zero tolerance policy is to prevent lenders from baiting borrowers with low initial estimates only to inflate fees at closing. Should a lender violate this rule by charging more at closing than what was initially quoted for these specific fees, they are required to reimburse the borrower for the difference. This ensures that borrowers can rely on the initial Loan Estimate as a true reflection of their closing costs, fostering trust and transparency in the lending process.

On the other hand, certain costs are subject to a 10% cumulative tolerance threshold. These costs include services the borrower can shop for but chooses to use providers on the lender's approved list, and recording fees. The cumulative aspect means that the total of all these costs can increase by up to 10% from the Loan Estimate to the Closing Disclosure. If the aggregate cost exceeds this 10% threshold, the lender must cover the excess, ensuring that borrowers are not unduly burdened by unexpected increases in these fees. This tolerance level acknowledges the variability in third-party services and recording fees, providing a buffer that accommodates legitimate fluctuations while still protecting the borrower from significant discrepancies.

Violation scenarios can arise when lenders fail to accurately estimate charges, leading to discrepancies between the Loan Estimate and the Closing Disclosure that exceed the prescribed tolerance levels. In such cases, lenders are obligated to refund the excess charges to the borrower at or before closing. This restitution is not merely a corrective action but serves as a deterrent against careless or deceptive estimation practices. It underscores the importance of diligence and integrity in the loan origination process, ensuring that lenders provide borrowers with accurate and reliable estimates from the outset.

Moreover, the regulations stipulate that lenders must provide a revised Loan Estimate if they become aware of changes to the estimated costs that exceed the tolerances allowed. This revision must be delivered to the borrower promptly, allowing for reevaluation and consent before proceeding to closing. This requirement for timely revision and disclosure further empowers borrowers, enabling them to make informed decisions based on the most current and accurate cost estimates.

The regulations governing accuracy and tolerances in service charges aim to safeguard consumers from unforeseen financial burdens resulting from inaccuracies in loan cost estimates. By mandating strict adherence to zero tolerance and 10% tolerance levels for specific charges, the regulations ensure that borrowers can trust the Loan Estimate provided by lenders. These measures promote transparency, accountability, and fairness in the mortgage lending process, aligning the interests of lenders and borrowers towards achieving a successful and equitable closing.

Disclosure Timing Rules

The **Know Before You Owe** initiative, also known as the TILA-RESPA Integrated Disclosure (TRID) rule, mandates specific timing for disclosures to ensure borrowers have ample time to review and understand the terms of their mortgage before proceeding to closing. The cornerstone of this regulation is the delivery of the **Loan Estimate** and **Closing Disclosure**, which are critical documents designed to provide transparency and facilitate comparison shopping among different loan offers.

For the **Loan Estimate**, lenders are required to deliver or place in the mail no later than the third business day after receiving the borrower's application. This document outlines the estimated interest rates, monthly payments, and closing costs for the mortgage. It serves as an initial summary of the loan terms that allows borrowers to compare offers from different lenders effectively. The timing of this disclosure is crucial as it gives borrowers the opportunity to review potential costs and negotiate better terms if necessary.

Following the Loan Estimate, the **Closing Disclosure** must be provided to the borrower at least three business days before loan consummation. This document finalizes the loan terms and provides detailed closing costs. The three-day review period ensures that borrowers have sufficient time to understand and question any changes from the original Loan Estimate, thus preventing surprises at closing. If significant changes occur after the Closing Disclosure has been provided, such as changes in APR beyond a specified tolerance, the addition of a prepayment penalty, or changes in the loan product, a new disclosure must be provided, and another three-business-day review period is triggered.

Notification of action taken is another critical aspect of disclosure timing. Under the Equal Credit Opportunity Act (ECOA), lenders are required to notify applicants of the action taken on their loan application within 30 days of receiving a completed application. This notification can be an approval, a counteroffer, or a denial. If denied, the lender must provide a Notice of Adverse Action, detailing the reasons for denial, which is essential for transparency and allows applicants to address any issues before reapplying.

Early disclosures are also significant, particularly in the context of adjustable-rate mortgages (ARMs). Lenders must provide borrowers with a CHARM (Consumer Handbook on Adjustable-Rate Mortgages) booklet and an ARM program disclosure at the time of application or before payment of a non-refundable fee. These disclosures ensure that borrowers are fully informed about the potential variations in their interest rate and payments over the life of the loan.

Affiliated Business Arrangements (ABA) disclosures are required under the Real Estate Settlement Procedures Act (RESPA) when a settlement service provider involved in a real estate transaction refers the consumer to an affiliate for another settlement service. The referring party must provide an ABA disclosure at the time of referral or within three business days following the referral, which must detail the relationship between the referral and the service provider, along with an estimate of the second provider's charges. This disclosure is vital for maintaining transparency and allowing consumers to make informed decisions about the services they choose to use.

The timing of disclosures in the mortgage process is structured to ensure that borrowers receive all necessary information to make informed decisions that align with their best interests. The regulations related to the Know Before You Owe initiative, notification of action taken, early disclosures, and Affiliated Business Arrangements (ABAs) are essential for promoting transparency and enhancing borrower comprehension throughout the loan origination process.

Loan Estimate Timing and Corrections

The timing of the Loan Estimate is a critical component of the mortgage application process, governed by the Truth in Lending Act (TILA) and the Real Estate Settlement Procedures Act (RESPA) as integrated by the TILA-RESPA Integrated Disclosure (TRID) rule. Upon receipt of a borrower's mortgage application, lenders are mandated to deliver a Loan Estimate within three business days. This document provides the borrower with detailed information about the estimated interest rates, monthly payments, and closing costs associated with the mortgage offer. It is designed to give borrowers a clear understanding of the loan terms and the financial commitment they are considering, enabling them to compare different lenders' offers effectively.

In instances where there are valid changes in circumstances affecting the borrower's loan costs, a Revised Loan Estimate may be issued. Changes that can justify a revised estimate include changes in loan amount, loan product, and discoveries from the appraisal that affect the value of the property. However, the issuance of a Revised Loan Estimate is also bound by timing restrictions. It must be delivered to the borrower no later than four business days before loan consummation. Importantly, if there are less than four business days between the time the revised circumstances are discovered and the closing date, the Revised Loan Estimate may not be issued, but the lender may reflect the changes in the Closing Disclosure.

The expiration of the Loan Estimate is another crucial aspect. Borrowers are typically required to indicate their intent to proceed with the loan offer within ten business days after the Loan Estimate is delivered. If the borrower does not express intent within this period, the lender may consider the offer expired, and any quoted terms and estimated costs may be subject to change. This mechanism ensures that lenders provide timely and accurate estimates and that borrowers have a reasonable but limited timeframe to make informed decisions based on those estimates.

Tolerance corrections are integral to ensuring accuracy and fairness in the loan estimation process. Certain costs in the Loan Estimate are subject to tolerances, meaning they cannot increase by more than a specified amount at closing. There are zero tolerance charges, such as lender origination fees, which cannot increase at all from the Loan Estimate to the Closing Disclosure. Then, there are costs that can increase by up to 10% in the aggregate, such as certain third-party services the borrower can shop for and recording fees. If the actual closing costs exceed these tolerance thresholds, the lender must refund the difference to the borrower at closing. This rule protects borrowers from unexpected increases in costs and encourages lenders to provide accurate estimates from the outset.

The regulatory framework surrounding the Loan Estimate timing, revisions, expiration, and tolerance corrections is designed to promote transparency, accuracy, and fairness in the mortgage lending process. By adhering to these regulations, lenders help ensure that borrowers are well-informed and protected against unexpected financial burdens, thereby facilitating a more trustworthy and efficient mortgage market.

Closing Disclosure & Counseling Info

The Closing Disclosure is a critical document in the mortgage loan origination process, serving as a final review of the loan terms, costs, and other financial details before the consummation of the loan. It is meticulously designed to ensure borrowers have a clear, comprehensive understanding of their mortgage obligations. This document aligns closely with the Loan Estimate, which borrowers receive early in the loan application process, allowing for a detailed comparison of initially quoted terms against final terms. The alignment between the Closing Disclosure and the Loan Estimate is paramount, as it provides a transparent mechanism for borrowers to verify that the loan terms have not substantially changed to their detriment.

Mandatory homeownership counseling information is another vital component that must be included in the Closing Disclosure. This requirement is rooted in the Dodd-Frank Wall Street Reform and Consumer Protection Act, which aims to provide borrowers with all necessary resources to make informed decisions. The counseling information is especially crucial for first-time homebuyers or those participating in certain government-backed loan programs, such as FHA or VA loans, where understanding the long-term financial commitment and implications of a mortgage is essential.

The timing of the Closing Disclosure is strictly regulated. Borrowers must receive this document at least three business days before the loan consummation. This cooling-off period is designed to give borrowers sufficient time to review the final terms, ask any remaining questions, and ensure they are fully comfortable with the commitment they are about to make. It's a critical juncture where the alignment of the Closing Disclosure with the Loan Estimate can be thoroughly evaluated, discrepancies can be addressed, and the borrower can seek clarification or renegotiation of terms if necessary.

The contents of the Closing Disclosure include, but are not limited to, the loan amount, interest rate, projected payments, costs at closing, and a detailed breakdown of closing costs, including lender and third-party fees. It also specifies, in clear terms, whether the interest rate is fixed or adjustable, outlines prepayment penalties if any, and delineates escrow account details for property taxes and homeowner's insurance, if applicable.

For the homeownership counseling information, the Closing Disclosure must provide contact details for counseling agencies approved by the U.S. Department of Housing and Urban Development (HUD). This information empowers borrowers to seek independent advice and counseling to better understand the rights, responsibilities, and potential risks associated with their mortgage. It underscores the commitment to ensuring that borrowers are not only well-informed but also have access to resources that can aid in their decision-making process.

In essence, the Closing Disclosure and the mandatory homeownership counseling information work in tandem to safeguard borrower interests, promote understanding, and ensure that borrowers are making well-informed decisions as they enter into mortgage agreements. This approach aligns with the broader objectives of transparency, consumer protection, and financial literacy in the mortgage lending process.

Qualification: Processing & Underwriting

Borrower Analysis: Evaluating Financial Health

Evaluating a borrower's financial health is a critical step in the mortgage loan origination process, requiring a detailed analysis of assets, liabilities, income, credit reports, and qualifying ratios such as Loan-to-Value (LTV) and Debt-to-Income (DTI). Additionally, adherence to the Ability-to-Repay (ATR) rules ensures that borrowers are only approved for loans they can feasibly manage, safeguarding both the lender and borrower from potential financial distress.

Assets provide a snapshot of the borrower's financial strength, including savings accounts, retirement accounts, real estate, and other investments. They offer insight into the borrower's ability to make a down payment, cover closing costs, and sustain mortgage payments in case of financial upheaval. Lenders meticulously verify the existence and stability of these assets, often requiring documentation such as bank statements and investment account summaries.

Liabilities, on the other hand, encompass all current debts and obligations, including car loans, credit card debt, student loans, and other personal loans. Evaluating liabilities is essential for understanding the borrower's existing financial commitments and determining their capacity to take on additional debt. Lenders calculate the monthly payments on these liabilities to assess their impact on the borrower's cash flow.

Income stability is a cornerstone of borrower analysis. Lenders scrutinize the borrower's income sources, including employment, self-employment, rental income, or income from investments. This evaluation not only verifies the current income level but also assesses its consistency and reliability over time. Employment verification letters, tax returns, and pay stubs are commonly requested documents in this process.

The **credit report** serves as a comprehensive record of the borrower's credit history, including past and present debts, payment history, and overall credit management. Credit scores, derived from these reports, play a pivotal role in determining the borrower's creditworthiness. A higher credit score indicates a lower risk to the lender, potentially qualifying the borrower for more favorable loan terms.

Qualifying ratios, specifically the LTV and DTI ratios, are critical metrics in the loan approval process. The **LTV ratio** compares the loan amount to the value of the property, reflecting the loan's risk level. A lower LTV ratio often results in more favorable loan conditions. The **DTI ratio**, which compares the borrower's total monthly debt payments to their gross monthly income, assesses the borrower's ability to manage monthly payments. Lenders typically seek a DTI ratio of 43% or lower, as mandated by the ATR requirements.

The **Ability-to-Repay (ATR) rules** require lenders to make a reasonable and good faith determination of the borrower's ability to repay the loan. This involves considering factors such as income, employment status, monthly mortgage payments, simultaneous loans, and mortgage-related obligations. Compliance with ATR rules is non-negotiable, ensuring that loans are only issued to borrowers with a demonstrated ability to manage their repayment obligations.

The borrower analysis phase is a multifaceted process that demands a thorough examination of financial documents and adherence to regulatory standards. By meticulously evaluating assets, liabilities, income stability, credit reports, and qualifying ratios, lenders can make informed decisions that align with both industry regulations and the financial well-being of the borrower. This rigorous analysis is fundamental to maintaining the integrity of the mortgage lending process and ensuring the long-term success of both the borrower and lender.

Appraisals: Purpose, Approaches, Timing

Appraisals serve a pivotal role in the mortgage loan origination process, providing a professional and unbiased estimate of a property's market value. This valuation is crucial for lenders to determine the loan-to-value ratio, a key factor in loan approval decisions and risk assessment. The primary purpose of an appraisal is to ensure that the mortgage loan amount does not exceed the property's worth, thereby mitigating the financial risk for lenders in the event of borrower default. Additionally, appraisals protect the borrower from overpaying for a property.

There are three main approaches to property appraisal: the market, income, and cost approaches. The market approach compares the subject property with similar properties that have recently sold in the same geographic area, taking into consideration factors such as location, size, condition, and features. Adjustments are made for differences between the properties to arrive at an estimated value. This approach is most commonly used for residential property appraisals.

The income approach is primarily used for investment or commercial properties and estimates value based on the income the property generates. This involves calculating the present value of future income streams, considering factors such as rental income, operating expenses, and vacancy rates. The capitalization rate, which is the rate of return expected on an investment property, plays a crucial role in this valuation method.

The cost approach estimates the value of a property by determining how much it would cost to replace or reproduce the property, minus depreciation. This approach considers the value of the land (assuming it's vacant) and adds the current cost to construct a building of similar size and utility. The cost approach is particularly useful for new properties or those with unique features that are not easily compared to other properties in the market.

Timing is critical in the appraisal process. Appraisals are typically conducted after the buyer and seller have agreed on a purchase price and a mortgage application has been filed. The appraisal must be completed before the loan can be approved to ensure the property value supports the loan amount. Lenders often require appraisals to be completed within a certain timeframe, usually within 30 days of the loan application, to ensure the valuation reflects the current market conditions.

The requirement for appraisal independence is mandated to prevent any undue influence or pressure on the appraiser that could affect the impartiality of the valuation. Regulations such as the Appraisal Independence Requirements (AIR) within the Dodd-Frank Wall Street Reform and Consumer Protection Act, and guidelines provided by the Federal Housing Finance Agency (FHFA), prohibit lenders from directly selecting appraisers or having direct contact with appraisers to discuss valuations. Instead, many lenders use an independent appraisal management company (AMC) to oversee the appraisal process. This ensures that the appraisal is conducted objectively, providing a fair and accurate assessment of the property's value.

Appraisals play a crucial role in the mortgage lending process, serving as a protective measure for both lenders and borrowers by confirming that the property value aligns with the loan amount. The choice of the appropriate appraisal method is influenced by the type of property and the specific purpose of the appraisal. Additionally, the timing and independence of the appraisal process are subject to regulations that ensure the integrity and accuracy of the valuation, which is vital for the effective origination of a mortgage loan.

Title Reports and Commitments

Obtaining a title report is a crucial step in the mortgage loan origination process, serving as a comprehensive document that details the legal status of real estate property. It includes information on the current owner, liens, encumbrances, easements, and any restrictions that may affect the property's title. Mortgage Loan Originators (MLOs) and underwriters rely on title reports to assess the risk associated with lending on a particular property and to ensure that the property's title can be transferred free of issues that could affect its marketability or the lender's lien position.

Timing for obtaining title reports is typically initiated once the mortgage application has moved into the underwriting stage and a property has been identified for purchase or refinance. The process involves contracting a title company or attorney to conduct a thorough search of public records to compile the title report. This search can reveal critical details such as prior deeds, court judgments, property and estate taxes, divorces, bankruptcy filings, or any other legal actions that might affect ownership. The timing is crucial as it allows any issues identified to be resolved before the loan closing. Generally, title reports should be obtained and reviewed well in advance of the closing date, often several weeks prior, to allow sufficient time for the resolution of any discovered issues.

Commitments for title insurance are typically issued after the preliminary title report is reviewed and any title defects have been cleared, or plans for their resolution have been made. This commitment is an agreement from the title insurance company to issue a title insurance policy after closing, protecting the lender (and possibly the borrower, if they opt for owner's coverage) against losses arising from undiscovered defects in the title that were not identified during the title search.

Verifying ownership and encumbrances involves a detailed examination of the title report to confirm the legal owner of the property and to identify any liens, loans, or other claims against the property that could affect the lender's security interest. Encumbrances can include mortgages, judgment liens, mechanic's liens, and tax liens. It's imperative for MLOs and underwriters to ensure these encumbrances are resolved or adequately managed before proceeding with the loan.

Reviewing preliminary title reports for closing readiness involves checking that all necessary documents and endorsements are in place for a smooth transfer of title. This includes ensuring that seller ownership is correctly established, all liens and encumbrances are accounted for or cleared, and any conditions for the issuance of title insurance are met. The preliminary report offers a snapshot of the title's current status, allowing the lender, buyer, and seller to address any potential issues early in the closing process.

In essence, the title report and the processes surrounding it are foundational to the mortgage lending process, ensuring that the property being financed is free of legal complications that could jeopardize the lender's investment or the borrower's ownership rights. MLOs play a critical role in coordinating these efforts, working closely with title companies, attorneys, and underwriters to navigate the complexities of title search and insurance, ultimately facilitating a secure and efficient closing process.

Insurance: Flood, PMI, Hazard, Government

In the realm of mortgage loan origination, understanding the nuances of various insurance requirements is pivotal for both Mortgage Loan Originators (MLOs) and prospective borrowers. Insurance, in its various forms, serves as a safeguard against potential financial losses for both the lender and the borrower. This section delves into the specifics of flood insurance, Private Mortgage Insurance (PMI), hazard/homeowner's insurance, and government mortgage insurance, elucidating their significance in the mortgage process.

Flood insurance is mandated by federal law for properties located in high-risk flood zones, as designated by the Federal Emergency Management Agency (FEMA). Lenders require flood insurance to protect the property, which serves as collateral for the mortgage, from loss or damage due to flooding. The requirement for flood insurance is triggered by the property's location within a Special Flood Hazard Area (SFHA) and remains in effect for the life of the loan. The cost of flood insurance varies depending on the property's risk level, coverage amount, and deductible chosen by the borrower. It's crucial for MLOs to inform borrowers about the necessity of flood insurance early in the loan application process to ensure compliance and to factor in the cost of premiums into their budgeting.

Private Mortgage Insurance (PMI) is required for conventional loans when the borrower makes a down payment of less than 20% of the home's purchase price, resulting in a Loan-to-Value

(LTV) ratio greater than 80%. PMI protects the lender against the borrower's default on the loan. The cost of PMI varies based on the down payment amount, loan term, and borrower's credit score. PMI can be canceled once the borrower has accumulated sufficient equity in the home, typically when the LTV ratio reaches 78% through a combination of principal reduction and property appreciation. MLOs must provide clear information on PMI, including how premiums are calculated, payment options, and the process for cancellation, to help borrowers make informed decisions.

Hazard or homeowner's insurance is required by lenders to protect the property against losses from fire, storms, theft, and other hazards. This insurance covers the cost of repairing or rebuilding the property and, in some cases, the replacement of personal possessions. Lenders require borrowers to maintain adequate coverage for the life of the loan, with the insurance premium often included in the monthly mortgage payment and placed in an escrow account. The amount of coverage and the premium depend on the property's value, location, and the borrower's chosen deductible. MLOs play a key role in ensuring borrowers understand the coverage requirements and how insurance premiums impact their overall mortgage payment.

Government mortgage insurance is a critical component for loans backed by the Federal Housing Administration (FHA) and the Department of Veterans Affairs (VA). FHA loans require a Mortgage Insurance Premium (MIP), which includes an upfront premium paid at closing and an annual premium divided into monthly payments. MIP is required regardless of the LTV ratio, providing protection to the lender against losses. VA loans do not require monthly mortgage insurance premiums; however, a one-time funding fee is charged at closing, the amount of which depends on the loan amount, type of service, and whether it's the borrower's first VA loan. Understanding the distinctions between FHA and VA mortgage insurance is essential for MLOs to guide borrowers through the financing options that best suit their needs.

Insurance in the mortgage process serves as a critical risk management tool, protecting the financial interests of both lenders and borrowers. MLOs must possess a comprehensive understanding of flood insurance, PMI, hazard/homeowner's insurance, and government mortgage insurance requirements to navigate borrowers through the complexities of mortgage financing, ensuring compliance and financial preparedness.

Closing

Title Insurance and Its Importance

Title insurance serves as a pivotal safeguard in the real estate transaction process, offering protection to both lenders and buyers against unforeseen defects in the title to a property that could result in financial loss. Unlike traditional insurance policies that protect against future events, title insurance provides coverage for past occurrences that may affect the title and ownership of the property. These may include issues such as errors in public records, undisclosed heirs claiming ownership, forgeries, easements, or encumbrances that were not previously identified.

The process of obtaining title insurance begins with a comprehensive search of public records by the title company. This search aims to identify any potential issues or defects with the property's title. Despite the thorough nature of this search, some risks may not be discoverable through public records alone, such as fraud or forgery. Title insurance protects against these and other hidden defects that could challenge the buyer's or lender's rights to the property.

There are two primary types of title insurance policies: the lender's policy and the owner's policy. The lender's policy is typically required by the mortgage lender and only protects the lender's interest in the property up to the amount of the mortgage loan. Conversely, the owner's policy is designed to protect the buyer's equity in the property. While the lender's policy is a mandatory requirement for securing a mortgage, the owner's policy is usually optional, though highly recommended for the protection it affords to the property owner.

The importance of title clarity before closing cannot be overstated. Clear title is essential for the legal transfer of property ownership. It ensures that the seller has the right to sell the property and that the buyer is acquiring a property free from title defects, liens, or other encumbrances, except those expressly agreed upon at the time of sale. Title clarity provides peace of mind to all parties involved in the transaction, facilitating a smoother closing process.

In the event of a title claim, the title insurance company will defend the insured party (either the lender or the owner) in court at no additional cost to the insured. If the claim proves valid, the title insurance company will compensate the insured up to the policy limit for financial loss incurred as a result of the defect in title.

The one-time premium for title insurance is paid at closing and is calculated based on the purchase price of the property or the amount of the loan. Considering the significant investment involved in purchasing property and the potential costs associated with defending a title claim, title insurance provides critical financial protection and peace of mind for both buyers and lenders in real estate transactions.

Settlement Agent & Valid Signatures

The settlement or closing agent plays a critical role in the final stages of the mortgage loan process, ensuring that the transfer of property is executed correctly and legally. This agent is responsible for coordinating all closing activities, including the collection and disbursement of funds, ensuring that the transaction adheres to all legal and financial requirements, and facilitating the signing of the closing documents. One of the key responsibilities of the settlement agent is to ensure that all signatures on the security instrument, typically a mortgage or deed of trust, are valid and legally binding.

Valid signatures are essential for the enforceability of the security instrument. These signatures must come from individuals who have the legal capacity to enter into a mortgage agreement. Typically, this includes all parties who hold title to the property and, in some cases, their spouses, depending on state law. The settlement agent must verify the identity of each signer to ensure that the individuals signing the documents are indeed who they claim to be. This verification process often involves checking government-issued identification and ensuring that the names on the ID match those on the closing documents.

The use of a power of attorney (POA) in closing is a situation that requires meticulous attention from the settlement agent. A POA is a legal document that grants one person the authority to act on behalf of another. In mortgage closings, a POA might be used if a borrower cannot be physically present to sign the closing documents. The individual granted this power, known as the attorney-in-fact, must act within the scope of authority specified in the POA document.

For a POA to be used at closing, the settlement agent must ensure that the document is valid and complies with state laws. This includes verifying that the POA grants the attorney-in-fact the specific powers needed to sign the closing documents, such as the power to enter into loan agreements or convey real property. The agent must also confirm that the POA is durable, meaning it remains in effect even if the principal becomes incapacitated, if applicable. Additionally, the settlement agent must verify that the POA has not been revoked and that the principal is alive at the time of closing, as the death of the principal automatically revokes the POA.

The settlement agent is responsible for ensuring that all documents signed under a POA are executed correctly. This involves checking that the attorney-in-fact signs the document in a manner that clearly indicates they are signing on behalf of the principal. For example, if John

Doe is signing as an attorney-in-fact for Jane Smith, he might sign as "Jane Smith, by John Doe, her attorney-in-fact." This clarity is crucial for the legal enforceability of the signed documents.

The settlement agent's role in verifying eligible signatures and overseeing the proper use of a power of attorney during the closing process is vital for the legal completion of the mortgage transaction. Ensuring that all signatures are valid and that any POA is correctly executed protects all parties involved in the transaction and helps to prevent future legal disputes over the validity of the mortgage or deed of trust.

Explanation of Closing Cost Components

Understanding the various components that contribute to the closing costs of a mortgage transaction is crucial for both mortgage loan originators and borrowers. These costs encompass a range of fees and expenses, each serving a specific purpose in the completion of a real estate transaction. Among these, the HUD-1 Settlement Statement, title insurance, pre-paid items, escrow expenses, and loan origination fees are pivotal.

The HUD-1 Settlement Statement, now more commonly integrated into the Closing Disclosure due to the TILA-RESPA Integrated Disclosure (TRID) rule changes, itemizes all charges imposed on borrowers and sellers during a real estate transaction. This document provides a detailed account of all transaction costs, ensuring transparency. It includes line-item representations of each fee, tax, and transfer charge, allowing parties to see precisely where their funds are allocated. For mortgage loan originators, a thorough understanding of each line item is essential to guide borrowers through their closing costs effectively.

Title insurance plays a dual role in protecting both the lender and the buyer against potential losses due to defects in the title of the property that were not discovered at the time of sale. The lender's policy safeguards the lender's interest up to the loan amount, while the owner's policy covers the buyer's equity in the property. The cost of title insurance varies based on the purchase price of the property and the loan amount but is a one-time fee paid at closing. It ensures that property rights are clear and undisputed, a fundamental aspect of securing the investment for all parties involved.

Pre-paid items are future costs related to the property that are paid in advance at closing. These typically include property taxes, homeowner's insurance, and mortgage insurance premiums. Lenders often require these payments to be made at closing to ensure that these critical expenses are covered from the outset, protecting both the borrower's and lender's interests in the property. The amounts for these pre-paid items are placed into an escrow account, from which the lender will pay the future bills as they come due.

Escrow expenses relate to the funds held in an escrow account to cover recurring costs associated with the property, including taxes and insurance. The initial escrow deposit at closing ensures that the lender has sufficient funds to pay these expenses on the borrower's behalf when they become due. The amount required to start the escrow account can vary depending on the timing of the closing and the specific requirements of the taxing authorities and insurance companies.

Loan origination fees are charged by the lender for processing the new loan application. These fees cover the lender's administrative costs, including credit checks, loan documentation preparation, and the loan approval process. Typically expressed as a percentage of the loan amount, origination fees are negotiable and vary by lender. Understanding how these fees are calculated and what they cover can help borrowers and mortgage loan originators negotiate the best possible terms.

A thorough understanding of the various components that contribute to closing costs is essential for mortgage professionals assisting their clients throughout the mortgage process. By clarifying these expenses, mortgage loan originators can offer important information to borrowers, ensuring they are well aware of how their funds are allocated and the necessity of these costs in securing their new home or investment property.

Required Closing Documents

At the culmination of the mortgage loan process, several critical documents must be prepared, reviewed, and signed to ensure the legal transfer of property and to secure the loan. Among these, the **promissory note**, **deed of trust**, **Closing Disclosure**, **title documents**, and **borrower identification** stand out as fundamental to closing.

The **promissory note** is a key financial document that outlines the borrower's promise to repay the loan. It specifies the loan amount, interest rate, payment schedule, and terms of repayment. This document is crucial because it represents the borrower's indebtedness and the lender's right to receive payments. The precise details, including the interest calculation method, whether simple or compound, and any provisions for late fees or prepayment penalties, are meticulously outlined. The promissory note is legally binding and enforceable in a court of law, making it essential for both parties to fully understand its terms.

Another vital document is the **deed of trust**, which serves as security for the loan. The deed of trust transfers legal title of the property to a trustee, who holds it as security for the loan. Should the borrower default on the loan, the trustee has the authority to sell the property to repay the lender. This document includes the identities of the borrower and lender, a legal description of the property, and the conditions under which the trustee can take possession of the property. The deed of trust is recorded in public records, creating a lien on the property.

The **Closing Disclosure** is a comprehensive statement of the loan terms, costs, and other critical information. It is designed to provide transparency to the borrower, detailing the final costs associated with the mortgage. This document includes the loan amount, interest rate, projected monthly payments, and a breakdown of closing costs and fees. Lenders are required to provide the Closing Disclosure to borrowers at least three business days before the loan closing date, allowing time for review and clarification of any terms.

Title documents are essential to establish and transfer ownership of the property. These include a title abstract, which provides the history of the property, including previous ownership, and any encumbrances or liens against the property. Title insurance policies, both lender's and owner's, are also key documents, offering protection against losses from title defects. Ensuring clear title is crucial for the legal transfer of property ownership and for the lender's security interest in the property.

Finally, **borrower identification** is required to verify the identity of the individuals entering into the loan agreement. Acceptable forms of identification typically include government-issued photo IDs, such as a driver's license or passport. This step is vital for compliance with laws designed to prevent fraud and money laundering.

Each of these documents plays a critical role in the mortgage closing process, serving to protect the interests of both the borrower and the lender. Their preparation, review, and execution are fundamental steps in ensuring the legality and success of the property transfer and loan agreement.

Funding Procedures and Rescission Periods

Upon the successful completion of the closing process, the funding phase commences, marking a critical juncture in the mortgage loan origination cycle. This phase is characterized by the disbursement of loan funds from the lender to the borrower, facilitating the transfer of property ownership or the refinancing of an existing mortgage. The timing of fund disbursements is governed by strict regulations to ensure the orderly execution of the mortgage transaction, safeguarding the interests of all parties involved.

The funding process typically begins immediately after all closing documents have been signed and all closing conditions have been satisfactorily met. However, the actual disbursement of funds may vary depending on the type of loan and the specific terms agreed upon between the borrower and the lender. For purchase transactions, lenders often disburse funds on the day of closing, allowing for the immediate transfer of property ownership. In contrast, refinancing transactions may be subject to mandatory waiting periods that delay the disbursement of funds.

One of the most significant regulatory provisions affecting the funding process is the right of rescission, which is applicable to certain types of mortgage refinancing and home equity loans. Under the Truth in Lending Act (TILA), borrowers are granted a 3-day rescission period, commencing from the finalization of the closing process. This period allows borrowers to reconsider their decision to refinance their mortgage or take out a home equity loan, providing a safeguard against hasty financial decisions. During this time, borrowers have the legal right to cancel the transaction without penalty, a provision that underscores the importance of informed decision-making in mortgage transactions.

The right of rescission applies exclusively to refinancing transactions involving the borrower's primary residence and does not extend to purchase transactions or refinancing involving investment properties or second homes. If a borrower decides to exercise their right of rescission, they must notify the lender in writing within the 3-day period. Upon receipt of the cancellation notice, the lender is obligated to refund any fees or costs paid by the borrower in connection with the loan application and closing process. The rescission period is a critical consumer protection feature that emphasizes transparency and borrower autonomy in the mortgage lending process.

Following the expiration of the rescission period, assuming the borrower has not exercised their right to cancel, the lender proceeds with the disbursement of funds. In refinancing transactions, this typically involves paying off the existing mortgage and any other debts or liens against the property, with any remaining funds disbursed directly to the borrower or used for other agreed-upon purposes. The precise timing of fund disbursement after the rescission period may vary, but lenders generally aim to complete the process as swiftly as regulatory compliance and operational procedures allow.

The funding process and the associated rescission period are integral components of the mortgage loan origination cycle, designed to ensure the orderly and equitable execution of mortgage transactions. By adhering to established timing rules and regulatory requirements, lenders and borrowers contribute to the overall integrity and efficiency of the mortgage lending ecosystem, facilitating successful property ownership and refinancing outcomes.

Financial Calculations

Calculating Periodic Interest

Calculating periodic interest is a fundamental aspect of understanding the financial implications of a mortgage loan. The periodic interest rate is the amount of interest charged on a loan balance for a specific period. It directly affects the total cost of the loan over its lifetime and determines the amount of each payment that goes towards interest versus principal reduction.

To calculate the periodic interest, you need to know the annual interest rate, the loan balance, and the payment frequency. The annual interest rate is typically provided as a percentage. Payment frequency refers to how often payments are made, commonly monthly, quarterly, or annually.

The formula to calculate the periodic interest amount is:

$$\text{Periodic Interest} = \frac{\text{Annual Interest Rate}}{\text{Number of Payments per Year}} \times \text{Loan Balance}$$

Let's break down each component:

- **Annual Interest Rate**: This is the interest rate charged on the loan balance, expressed as a percentage of the principal.
- **Number of Payments per Year**: This reflects how often payments are made. For monthly payments, this would be 12, quarterly would be 4, and annually would be 1.
- **Loan Balance**: The current outstanding balance of the loan.

For example, if you have a loan balance of $200,000 with an annual interest rate of 6% and payments are made monthly, the calculation for the monthly interest would be:

$$\text{Periodic Interest} = \frac{0.06}{12} \times 200{,}000 = \$1{,}000$$

This means that for each month, $1,000 of your payment will go towards interest. Understanding this calculation is crucial for mortgage loan originators and borrowers alike, as it impacts how quickly the principal balance of the loan decreases over time.

The impact of periodic interest on the total loan cost is significant. Loans with higher interest rates or more frequent payment schedules will accrue interest more rapidly, increasing the total amount of money paid over the life of the loan. Conversely, loans with lower interest rates and less frequent payment schedules will accrue interest more slowly, resulting in a lower total loan cost.

It's also important to note that as the loan balance decreases with each payment, the portion of each payment that goes towards interest will decrease, while the portion going towards the principal increases. This is due to the interest being calculated on the remaining loan balance, which diminishes over time as payments are made.

Understanding how to calculate periodic interest and its impact on the total loan cost is essential for making informed decisions about mortgage loans. It allows borrowers to compare different loan offers and choose the one that best suits their financial situation, ultimately influencing their ability to achieve financial freedom and flexibility.

Monthly Payment Calculations

Calculating monthly payments for a mortgage is a critical step in understanding the financial obligations of a home loan. The monthly payment is determined by several factors, including the loan term, the interest rate, and the principal amount of the loan. To accurately calculate this, one can use the formula for a fixed-rate mortgage, which is commonly represented as:

$$M = P \frac{r(1+r)^n}{(1+r)^n - 1}$$

Where:
- M is the total monthly mortgage payment.
- P is the principal loan amount.
- r is the monthly interest rate, derived from the annual rate divided by 12.
- n is the number of payments (loan term in years multiplied by 12).

This formula encapsulates the core components of a mortgage payment, providing a clear picture of the borrower's financial commitment over the term of the loan. The principal part of the loan is the amount borrowed from the lender, which will decrease over the term of the loan as payments are made. The interest rate, agreed upon at the initiation of the loan, directly influences the monthly payment amount; a higher interest rate results in higher monthly payments.

The breakdown of the monthly payment into principal and interest components is dynamic; initially, a larger portion of the monthly payment is allocated towards interest. Over time, as the principal balance decreases, the interest portion of the monthly payment decreases, while the principal portion increases. This is a fundamental concept known as amortization.

To illustrate, consider a $300,000 loan with a 30-year term (360 months) at an annual interest rate of 4%. The monthly interest rate (r) would be $\frac{4\%}{12} = 0.003333$. Plugging the values into the formula gives:

$$M = 300,000 \frac{0.003333(1 + 0.003333)^{360}}{(1 + 0.003333)^{360} - 1}$$

Solving this equation yields a monthly payment of approximately $1,432.25. This payment is fixed for the duration of the loan, assuming a fixed-rate mortgage. It's important to note that this calculation does not include taxes, homeowners insurance, or private mortgage insurance (PMI), which could significantly increase the monthly financial obligation.

Understanding the breakdown of each payment is crucial for mortgage loan originators when advising clients. It allows borrowers to see how much of their payment is going towards reducing the loan's principal versus paying interest to the lender. Additionally, it highlights the long-term cost of borrowing and the importance of considering the total interest paid over the life of the loan, not just the monthly payment or the interest rate.

This detailed approach to calculating and understanding monthly mortgage payments equips both mortgage professionals and borrowers with the knowledge to make informed decisions regarding loan options, terms, and overall financial planning in the context of home ownership.

Calculating Required Down Payments

Calculating the required down payment for a mortgage is a fundamental step in the loan origination process, directly influencing the borrower's financial commitment and the loan's overall cost. The down payment is the initial upfront portion of the total purchase price that the buyer pays out of pocket, not financed through the mortgage. It is crucial in determining the loan-to-value (LTV) ratio, a key risk assessment metric used by lenders to evaluate the loan's risk level. The LTV ratio is calculated by dividing the loan amount by the property's appraised value or purchase price, whichever is lower, and expressing the result as a percentage.

The formula for calculating the LTV ratio is as follows:

$$LTV = \left(\frac{\text{Loan Amount}}{\text{Property Value or Purchase Price}} \right) \times 100$$

To determine the required down payment, one must first understand the maximum LTV ratio allowed for the loan type they are considering. Different loan programs have varying LTV requirements, reflecting the lender's risk tolerance. For instance, conventional loans typically allow a maximum LTV ratio of 80%, meaning the borrower must make a down payment of at least 20% to avoid private mortgage insurance (PMI). Conversely, government-backed loans like FHA, VA, and USDA loans may permit higher LTV ratios, allowing for smaller down payments.

Given the property value or purchase price and the maximum LTV ratio for the loan type, the minimum required down payment can be calculated by rearranging the LTV formula to solve for the loan amount and then subtracting this from the property value or purchase price. The resulting formula for the down payment is:

$$\text{Down Payment} = \text{Property Value or Purchase Price} - \left(\text{Property Value or Purchase Price} \times \frac{\text{Maximum LTV Ratio}}{100}\right)$$

For example, for a $300,000 home with a conventional loan requiring a 20% down payment (or an 80% LTV ratio), the calculation would be:

$$\text{Down Payment} = 300{,}000 - \left(300{,}000 \times \frac{80}{100}\right) = 300{,}000 - 240{,}000 = 60{,}000$$

Thus, the borrower would need to provide a $60,000 down payment to secure the loan, reducing the financed amount and, consequently, the monthly mortgage payments. This upfront financial commitment also serves to reduce the lender's risk by ensuring the borrower has a significant personal investment in the property, aligning the interests of both parties.

The role of the down payment extends beyond just affecting the LTV ratio and monthly payments; it also influences the overall cost of the loan. A larger down payment reduces the amount borrowed, leading to lower interest costs over the life of the loan. Additionally, by lowering the LTV ratio, borrowers can avoid or minimize costs associated with PMI or other risk mitigation premiums required by lenders.

Understanding the intricacies of down payments, including how they are calculated and their impact on the loan's terms and costs, is essential for mortgage loan originators advising clients. It enables them to provide valuable guidance on selecting the most appropriate loan products and strategies for managing upfront costs, ultimately helping borrowers make informed decisions that align with their financial goals and capabilities.

Estimating Closing Costs and Prepaids

Estimating closing costs and prepaids is a critical component of the mortgage loan origination process, directly impacting the borrower's cash-to-close requirements. These costs encompass a variety of fees and expenses associated with finalizing a mortgage loan, and understanding their composition is essential for both mortgage professionals and borrowers. Closing costs can be broadly categorized into lender fees, prepaid items, escrow funding, and other miscellaneous expenses. Each of these categories plays a significant role in the overall financial picture of obtaining a mortgage.

Lender fees typically include loan origination charges, underwriting fees, and processing fees. These are costs that the lender assesses for the work involved in preparing, evaluating, and finalizing the loan. The exact amount can vary significantly based on the lender and the specific loan product. For instance, loan origination fees are often calculated as a percentage of the loan amount, commonly ranging from 0.5% to 1%. To calculate this, the formula $\text{Loan Origination Fee} = \text{Loan Amount} \times \text{Percentage Fee}$ is applied. For a loan amount of $300,000 with a 1% origination fee, the calculation would be $300,000 \times 0.01 = $3,000.

Prepaid items are costs that the borrower must pay at closing to cover expenses that will be incurred in the future but are related to the property or loan. These typically include homeowners insurance premiums, property taxes, and mortgage interest that accrues from the date of closing to the first mortgage payment. The amount required for prepaids will depend on the specific due dates and amounts of these expenses. For example, if property taxes are $6,000 annually and homeowners insurance is $1,200 annually, the borrower might need to prepay for several months of these costs upfront.

Escrow funding is closely related to prepaids but specifically refers to the initial deposit into an escrow account that the lender will use to pay future recurring costs such as taxes and insurance on behalf of the borrower. The initial escrow deposit calculation typically considers several months of property taxes and insurance premiums to ensure sufficient funds are available to cover these expenses when they are due. The formula for calculating the initial escrow deposit can vary, but a common approach is to take the total annual costs of taxes and insurance, divide by 12 to get a monthly amount, and then multiply by the number of months the lender requires to be held in escrow.

Other miscellaneous expenses can include title search and insurance fees, appraisal fees, credit report fees, and government recording charges. Title insurance fees, for example, protect against any legal issues that might arise from discrepancies in the property's title, and their cost is based on the purchase price of the property or the loan amount.

To accurately estimate the total closing costs, mortgage professionals compile these various fees and prepaids into a comprehensive overview, often utilizing a Loan Estimate form, which provides a detailed breakdown of anticipated costs. This document is crucial for borrowers to understand their total cash-to-close requirements, which include down payment plus all closing costs and prepaids. The total estimated closing costs can significantly affect the affordability and feasibility of the loan for the borrower, making accurate estimation and clear communication of these costs essential in the mortgage loan origination process.

ARM Adjustments: Rates and Payments

Adjustable-Rate Mortgages (ARMs) present a unique financial calculation challenge due to their variable interest rates. The recalibration of payments following an interest rate adjustment is a critical process for both mortgage loan originators and borrowers to understand. This recalibration hinges on several key components: the index, margin, interest rate caps, and the remaining loan balance.

The interest rate of an ARM is adjusted based on a specific benchmark or **index** plus a set **margin**. Common indices include the 1-year Constant-Maturity Treasury (CMT) securities, the London Interbank Offered Rate (LIBOR), and the Secured Overnight Financing Rate (SOFR). The **margin** is a fixed percentage point added to the index to determine the new interest rate. For example, if the index rate is 1.5% and the margin is 2.5%, the adjusted interest rate would be 4%.

Interest rate **caps** play a crucial role in limiting how much the interest rate can change during each adjustment period and over the life of the loan. Caps are typically articulated as per-adjustment caps, which limit the interest rate change at each adjustment period, and lifetime caps, which limit the total interest rate change over the loan's life.

To recalculate the monthly payment after an interest rate adjustment, one must first determine the new interest rate by adding the index rate to the margin, ensuring that this new rate adheres to the predetermined caps. Once the new rate is established, it is applied to the remaining loan balance to calculate the new monthly payment.

The formula for recalculating the monthly payment is as follows:

$$M = P \frac{r(1+r)^n}{(1+r)^n - 1}$$

Where:
- M is the new monthly payment.
- P is the remaining loan balance.
- r is the new monthly interest rate (annual interest rate divided by 12).
- n is the number of remaining payments.

For instance, consider an ARM with a remaining balance of $200,000, a remaining term of 240 months (20 years), and an interest rate adjustment to 4% (or 0.04 annual rate). The monthly interest rate (r) would be $\frac{0.04}{12} = 0.003333$. Plugging these values into the formula gives:

$$M = 200,000 \frac{0.003333(1 + 0.003333)^{240}}{(1 + 0.003333)^{240} - 1}$$

This calculation yields a new monthly payment, which reflects the adjusted interest rate applied to the remaining balance over the remaining term of the loan.

It is essential for mortgage professionals to adeptly navigate these recalculations to provide accurate and timely information to borrowers. Understanding the mechanics of ARM adjustments enables borrowers to anticipate changes in their financial obligations and plan accordingly. This knowledge is particularly crucial in environments of fluctuating interest rates, where adjustments can significantly impact monthly payments and overall loan costs.

Chapter 5: Ethics

Ethical Issues

Prohibited Acts and MLO Duties

Redlining, a discriminatory practice where services are denied or priced differently for residents in certain areas based on race or ethnicity, poses significant legal and ethical risks. This practice not only violates the Fair Housing Act but also undermines the principles of equality and fairness in the mortgage industry. Mortgage Loan Originators (MLOs) must ensure that loan products and services are offered to all eligible applicants on equal terms, without consideration of race, color, national origin, religion, sex, familial status, or disability. The consequences of engaging in or being complicit with redlining can include severe legal penalties, loss of licensure, and irreparable damage to professional reputation.

The Real Estate Settlement Procedures Act (RESPA) prohibits kickbacks and unearned fees in the mortgage lending process. Specifically, Section 8 of RESPA makes it illegal to give or accept any fee, kickback, or thing of value in exchange for referrals of settlement service business related to a federally related mortgage loan. MLOs must be vigilant to ensure that all compensation agreements for services rendered are for actual services performed and are reasonable and customary. Violations of RESPA can lead to enforcement actions, including fines, imprisonment, and civil liability.

Compensation for MLOs is another area heavily regulated to ensure fairness and transparency in the mortgage lending process. The Dodd-Frank Wall Street Reform and Consumer Protection Act, specifically through the Loan Originator Compensation rule enforced by the Consumer Financial Protection Bureau (CFPB), restricts the manner in which MLOs can be compensated. The rule prohibits compensation based on the terms of the transaction or a proxy for a term, such as the interest rate of the loan. Instead, compensation agreements must be based on a fixed percentage of the loan amount, a flat fee, or other non-prohibited bases. This regulation aims to prevent steering consumers into higher-cost or riskier loans that benefit the originator at the expense of the consumer.

MLOs have a duty to conduct their activities within the confines of these ethical and legal standards. This includes providing accurate and complete information to borrowers, ensuring that all fees and charges are justified and properly disclosed, and avoiding any actions that could be construed as discriminatory or unfair. MLOs should also be aware of their responsibilities under other relevant laws and regulations, such as the Equal Credit Opportunity Act (ECOA) and the Truth in Lending Act (TILA), which provide additional protections against discriminatory practices and require clear disclosure of loan terms.

In navigating these complex regulatory landscapes, MLOs must be diligent in their adherence to ethical practices and legal standards. This includes ongoing education and training to stay informed of changes in laws and regulations, implementing robust compliance programs within their organizations, and fostering a culture of integrity and fairness. By adhering to these principles, MLOs not only protect themselves from legal and regulatory risks but also contribute to a more equitable and trustworthy mortgage industry.

Fair Lending Practices and Compliance

Fair lending practices are foundational to maintaining integrity and trust within the mortgage industry. These practices are governed by several federal laws designed to ensure that all consumers have equal access to mortgage loans and services without discrimination based on race, color, religion, national origin, sex, marital status, age, or receipt of income from public assistance programs. A critical aspect of fair lending is the management of referrals, particularly in how mortgage loan originators (MLOs) interact with appraisers, real estate agents, and other third parties involved in the loan origination process.

Referrals in the mortgage industry must be handled with transparency and without any implication of kickbacks or fee splitting that could influence the impartiality of the service provided. The Real Estate Settlement Procedures Act (RESPA) requires that any business referral among settlement service providers be made without the expectation or exchange of any fee, kickback, or thing of value. MLOs must disclose any affiliated business arrangements to the borrower, detailing the relationship between the referral parties and the estimated charge or range of charges by the affiliate. This disclosure ensures that borrowers are fully informed and can make decisions based on transparent and fair information.

Coercion or any form of undue influence exerted on appraisers to manipulate property valuations undermines the integrity of the mortgage process and violates ethical standards and federal regulations. The Dodd-Frank Wall Street Reform and Consumer Protection Act, along with the Interagency Appraisal and Evaluation Guidelines, emphasize the importance of independent and objective appraisal services. MLOs must avoid any actions that could be perceived as pressuring appraisers to reach a predetermined valuation. Such practices not only compromise the fairness of the lending process but also can lead to significant legal and financial repercussions for the involved parties.

Discrimination in lending, whether overt or through policies and practices that have a discriminatory effect, is prohibited under the Equal Credit Opportunity Act (ECOA) and the Fair Housing Act. MLOs must ensure that all borrowers are evaluated based on their creditworthiness, without consideration of prohibited factors. Compliance with these laws involves regular training, monitoring of loan approval and denial patterns, and the implementation of fair lending policies that promote equality and prevent discriminatory practices.

Ensuring fairness in lending extends beyond compliance with legal requirements. It involves fostering a culture of ethical behavior and responsibility among MLOs and all participants in the mortgage industry. By prioritizing fair lending practices, the industry can uphold its commitment to providing equitable access to credit, thereby supporting the broader goal of homeownership and financial stability for all consumers.

Fraud Detection and Red Flags

In the realm of mortgage lending, vigilance against fraud is paramount to maintaining ethical standards and protecting the interests of all parties involved. Fraud detection encompasses a broad spectrum of activities, including the scrutiny of assets, income, employment verification, and the evaluation of sales contracts and applications for inconsistencies that may indicate fraudulent activity. Recognizing and understanding these red flags are critical skills for mortgage loan originators (MLOs) to ensure the integrity of the mortgage process.

Asset, income, and employment fraud often manifest through inflated or fictitious claims on a borrower's application. MLOs should be adept at verifying the authenticity of documents provided by borrowers. This includes cross-referencing income statements with tax returns, contacting employers directly to confirm employment status and salary, and scrutinizing bank statements for irregular deposits that may not be consistent with stated income. The use of third-party verification services can also be instrumental in identifying discrepancies that may signal fraudulent activity.

Sales contract and application inconsistencies serve as another significant red flag. MLOs should be alert to inconsistencies or alterations in the sales contract, such as seller contributions or alterations made without proper authorization. The presence of non-arms-length transactions, where the buyer and seller have a personal relationship that could unduly influence the sale price, requires careful examination. Additionally, applications that appear to have been tampered with, or contain inconsistent information about the borrower's financial situation or the property details, necessitate further investigation.

Occupancy fraud is another area of concern, where borrowers misrepresent their intention regarding the use of the property. This type of fraud typically involves a borrower claiming they intend to occupy the property as their primary residence to secure more favorable loan terms, when they actually intend to use it as an investment property. Indicators of occupancy fraud include the borrower's inability to provide reasonable explanations for purchasing a property in a location far removed from their current employment or having a rental agreement in place shortly after the loan closes.

General fraud indicators encompass a range of behaviors and document discrepancies that MLOs should be attuned to. These include but are not limited to, rapid re-applications after a recent denial, the use of PO boxes instead of physical addresses, discrepancies between the borrower's credit report and disclosed debts, and the involvement of parties to the transaction who have a history of fraudulent activity. Additionally, applications that seem to be rushed, with pressure to close quickly without adequate time for due diligence, may also signal potential fraud.

MLOs play a crucial role in fraud prevention, requiring a keen eye for detail and a thorough understanding of the mortgage process. By remaining vigilant and adhering to strict verification processes, MLOs can help safeguard the integrity of the mortgage industry and protect consumers from the detrimental effects of fraudulent activities.

Identifying Suspicious Bank Activities

Identifying suspicious transactions within the banking sector is a critical component of maintaining ethical standards in mortgage lending. Mortgage Loan Originators (MLOs) must be vigilant in observing and reporting any activities that deviate from normal banking practices, which could indicate potential fraud or money laundering. This includes, but is not limited to, unusual patterns of deposits or withdrawals, transactions involving large sums of money with no clear purpose, and any activity that seems to be structured to avoid reporting requirements.

Withholding material facts from borrowers, whether intentionally or through negligence, undermines the trust and transparency essential to the mortgage process. MLOs are obligated to ensure that all relevant information is provided to borrowers, enabling them to make informed decisions. This includes disclosing the terms of the loan, any risks associated with the mortgage product, and any changes to the loan terms as the application process progresses. Failure to do so not only violates ethical standards but also regulatory requirements, potentially leading to legal repercussions for both the individual MLO and their employing institution.

Verifying application information is a cornerstone of due diligence in mortgage lending. MLOs must undertake a thorough review of all information provided by the borrower, including employment verification, income assessment, and the source of down payment funds. This process often involves cross-referencing application details with external documents, such as tax returns, bank statements, and employer confirmation. Accuracy in this verification process is paramount, as it protects against loan fraud and ensures that borrowers are not approved for loans they cannot afford, thereby preventing potential financial distress or foreclosure.

In the context of suspicious banking activities, MLOs should be familiar with the red flags that may indicate illicit activities. These include transactions that do not fit the typical pattern of the borrower's financial behavior, abrupt changes in account balances without a plausible explanation, and the use of third parties to conduct transactions that would normally be expected to be done directly by the borrower. When such activities are detected, MLOs must follow established protocols for reporting these suspicions to the appropriate regulatory or law enforcement bodies.

Furthermore, MLOs play a crucial role in preventing the withholding of material facts from borrowers. This requires a commitment to transparency and the provision of complete and accurate information at all stages of the loan process. MLOs should ensure that borrowers understand the implications of their loan terms, including interest rates, repayment obligations, and any penalties for early repayment or default.

The verification of application information is not only a regulatory requirement but also a best practice that safeguards the integrity of the mortgage industry. MLOs should employ rigorous verification techniques, including direct contact with employers, the use of third-party verification services, and the careful analysis of financial documents. By doing so, MLOs contribute to the prevention of fraud and the promotion of responsible lending practices.

The identification of suspicious banking activities, the avoidance of withholding material facts from borrowers, and the meticulous verification of application information are essential duties of Mortgage Loan Originators. These practices are foundational to ethical conduct in the mortgage industry, ensuring the protection of consumers, the integrity of the mortgage process, and the stability of the financial system.

Advertising Compliance and UDAAP Standards

In the realm of mortgage lending, advertising serves as a critical bridge connecting Mortgage Loan Originators (MLOs) with potential clients. However, the integrity of this connection hinges on the adherence to ethical standards and regulatory compliance, particularly in avoiding misleading information, conducting due diligence, and preventing unfair, deceptive, or abusive acts as outlined by Unfair, Deceptive, or Abusive Acts or Practices (UDAAP) standards.

Ensuring federal compliance in marketing activities not only fosters trust among consumers but also upholds the reputation of the financial institution involved.

Misleading information in advertising can range from presenting incomplete loan cost details to suggesting approval guarantees that are not substantiated. To circumvent the dissemination of misleading claims, MLOs must ensure that all advertising content is transparent, providing a clear and comprehensive representation of loan terms, costs, and the borrower's obligations. This involves a meticulous review of advertising materials to verify that they do not exaggerate the benefits or omit critical information that could mislead consumers about the nature of the product offered.

Conducting due diligence in advertising practices entails a proactive approach to verify that all claims made in advertisements are accurate and supported by current product offerings and terms. This process includes regular audits of marketing materials and campaigns to ensure consistency with the institution's approved product descriptions and terms. It also involves training for staff involved in marketing and sales to understand the regulatory requirements governing mortgage advertising, thereby preventing inadvertent dissemination of misleading information.

Adhering to UDAAP standards requires a commitment to fairness and integrity in all consumer interactions. This commitment is demonstrated through advertising that respects the consumer's right to clear and factual information. It involves avoiding tactics that could manipulate or coerce consumers into making financial decisions that may not be in their best interest. MLOs must be vigilant against practices that could be perceived as unfair, deceptive, or abusive, such as using high-pressure sales tactics or providing incomplete information that could lead to misunderstandings about loan terms.

Federal regulation of mortgage advertising is comprehensive, encompassing various laws and regulations designed to protect consumers. The Truth in Lending Act (TILA), for instance, mandates clear disclosure of loan terms and costs, while the Mortgage Acts and Practices – Advertising Rule (MAP-AD Rule) specifically targets misleading claims in mortgage advertising. Compliance with these regulations requires a thorough understanding of the legal landscape governing mortgage lending and advertising. MLOs and their employing institutions must stay informed about regulatory changes and updates to ensure ongoing compliance.

Ensuring federal compliance in marketing also involves implementing internal controls and procedures for creating, reviewing, and approving advertising materials. This may include the establishment of a compliance review team responsible for vetting all advertising content before its release. Such measures not only help in preventing regulatory violations but also in building consumer confidence in the institution's commitment to ethical practices.

Avoiding misleading claims, conducting due diligence on advertisements, adhering to UDAAP standards, and ensuring compliance with federal regulations are fundamental to ethical advertising practices in the mortgage industry. These practices are not merely regulatory requirements but are also crucial to maintaining the trust and confidence of consumers, thereby supporting the integrity and success of the mortgage lending ecosystem.

Predatory Lending and Steering Practices

Predatory lending and steering represent two of the most egregious ethical violations within the mortgage industry, directly contravening the principles of fairness, transparency, and responsibility that should guide all mortgage loan originators (MLOs). Predatory lending involves imposing unfair and abusive loan terms on borrowers. Typically, these practices include exorbitant interest rates, high fees, and loan terms that are deliberately structured to result in the borrower's default, leading to foreclosure. Steering, on the other hand, involves guiding borrowers towards specific loans not because they are the most suitable for their needs, but because they are more profitable for the loan originator or lender, often disregarding the borrower's ability to repay.

To combat predatory lending, MLOs must adhere to a strict code of ethics and legal compliance, ensuring that all loan products offered are in the best interest of the borrower, taking into account their financial situation, objectives, and ability to repay the loan. This involves a comprehensive assessment of the borrower's financial health, including income, debt, credit history, and long-term financial goals. MLOs must provide a transparent explanation of all loan terms, including interest rates, payment structure, fees, and any penalties for late payments or default. This transparency ensures that borrowers are fully informed and can make decisions based on accurate and complete information.

In addressing the issue of steering, MLOs must present a range of loan options to borrowers, clearly outlining the benefits and drawbacks of each. This presentation should be unbiased, allowing the borrower to make an informed choice based on their specific needs and circumstances. MLOs should avoid any practices that could be construed as coercive or manipulative, such as withholding information about certain loan products or exaggerating the benefits of more profitable loans.

To ensure that products meet borrower needs and abilities, MLOs should engage in open and honest communication with borrowers throughout the loan process. This includes answering questions clearly and concisely, providing detailed explanations of complex loan terms, and offering guidance on how different loan options may impact the borrower's financial future. MLOs should also be proactive in identifying any potential issues that may arise during the loan term, such as changes in interest rates for adjustable-rate mortgages or the implications of balloon payments, and discuss these with the borrower to ensure they are prepared for any eventualities.

Regulatory compliance plays a critical role in preventing predatory lending and steering. MLOs must be thoroughly familiar with all relevant laws and regulations, including the Truth in Lending Act (TILA), the Real Estate Settlement Procedures Act (RESPA), and the Dodd-Frank Wall Street Reform and Consumer Protection Act, among others. These regulations provide a framework for ethical lending practices, including requirements for disclosure, fair lending, and consumer protection. MLOs must ensure that all loans originated comply with these regulations, conducting regular audits and reviews to identify and correct any deviations from legal and ethical standards.

Preventing predatory lending and steering necessitates a dedication to ethical practices, adherence to regulations, and a focus on the needs of borrowers in mortgage lending. Prioritizing the interests and requirements of borrowers enables MLOs to maintain the integrity of the mortgage industry, build trust with consumers, and support the overall stability of the housing market.

Ethical Behavior in Loan Origination

Financial Responsibility and Fee Regulations

In the realm of mortgage loan origination, financial responsibility encompasses a broad spectrum of practices, including the management of permitted fees and compensation, the ethical handling of fee changes, and the strict adherence to regulations governing closing cost scenarios, referral fees, and fee splitting. Mortgage Loan Originators (MLOs) must navigate these aspects with precision and integrity, ensuring compliance with both federal and state laws to maintain the trust of borrowers and uphold the reputation of the lending institution.

Permitted Fees and Compensation practices are defined by regulatory authorities such as the Consumer Financial Protection Bureau (CFPB). MLOs are allowed to receive compensation that is directly related to the services they provide. This compensation must not vary based on the loan terms or conditions, with the exception of the amount of credit extended. For instance, an MLO can be compensated based on a percentage of the loan amount, which is a common practice in the industry. However, the compensation structure must be clearly outlined in the MLO's agreement with their employer and disclosed to the borrower in compliance with the Truth in Lending Act (TILA) and Regulation Z.

Disclosing Fee Changes is a critical aspect of transparency and ethical conduct in mortgage loan origination. Any changes to fees, whether they are lender-imposed or third-party fees, must be communicated to the borrower as soon as possible. The Loan Estimate form, required by the TILA-RESPA Integrated Disclosure (TRID) rule, provides an initial disclosure of fees. Subsequent changes that occur must be re-disclosed to the borrower, ensuring that they are fully informed throughout the loan process. Significant changes may necessitate the issuance of a revised Loan Estimate, and certain changes may trigger a new three-day review period before loan consummation.

Closing Cost Scenarios must be accurately represented to borrowers, detailing all expected costs associated with the mortgage. This includes lender fees, title insurance, appraisal fees, and any prepaid items such as property taxes and homeowner's insurance. MLOs play a crucial role in ensuring that closing cost estimates are as accurate as possible, minimizing surprises at closing. The use of tolerances as defined by TRID helps to ensure that actual closing costs do not exceed the amounts disclosed to the borrower by significant margins.

Referral Fees and Fee Splitting are areas where strict regulations are in place to prevent unethical practices. The Real Estate Settlement Procedures Act (RESPA) prohibits the payment or acceptance of fees, kickbacks, or anything of value in exchange for the referral of settlement service business. This includes referrals between MLOs and real estate agents, title companies, or appraisers. Fee splitting, where two or more parties split a fee for services not actually rendered, is also prohibited under RESPA. MLOs must avoid any arrangements that could be construed as a kickback or fee splitting, ensuring that all compensation is for actual services provided.

In conclusion, maintaining financial responsibility in loan origination requires MLOs to adhere to established regulations governing fees, compensation, and referrals. By ensuring transparency, accuracy, and ethical practices in all financial dealings, MLOs contribute to the integrity of the mortgage lending process, fostering trust among borrowers and compliance with regulatory standards.

Handling Borrower Complaints

Addressing borrower complaints promptly and effectively is a critical component of ethical behavior in loan origination. When a complaint is received, it is essential to acknowledge it immediately, providing the borrower with a timeline for investigation and resolution. This initial step not only demonstrates respect for the borrower's concerns but also sets the stage for a transparent resolution process.

Documenting the complaint thoroughly is the next critical step. This involves recording the borrower's concerns in detail, including the date the complaint was received, the nature of the complaint, and any relevant communication or transactions leading up to the issue. Documentation should be meticulous, creating a comprehensive record that can be referred to throughout the resolution process. This record is invaluable not only for resolving the current issue but also for identifying patterns that might indicate systemic problems requiring broader solutions.

Ensuring resolution of the complaint involves investigating the issue thoroughly to understand the root cause. This may require reviewing loan files, discussing the matter with involved staff, and verifying compliance with all applicable laws and regulations. The goal is to identify not only how to resolve the specific complaint but also how to prevent similar issues in the future. Solutions might involve correcting errors, providing additional information, or other actions to address the borrower's concerns satisfactorily.

Compliance with regulatory requirements is a non-negotiable aspect of handling complaints. This includes adhering to timelines for complaint resolution set by laws and regulations, ensuring that any resolution is in compliance with applicable laws, and reporting the complaint and its resolution as required by regulatory bodies. For example, the Consumer Financial Protection Bureau (CFPB) and state regulatory agencies may have specific requirements for complaint handling, including timelines for acknowledgment and resolution, as well as requirements for reporting and record-keeping.

Throughout this process, communication with the borrower is key. Borrowers should be kept informed of the progress of their complaint, including any findings from the investigation and steps being taken towards resolution. Clear, consistent communication can help maintain trust and can prevent misunderstandings that could further complicate the resolution process.

Handling borrower complaints with promptness, thorough documentation, and a commitment to resolution is vital for upholding ethical standards in loan origination. This method not only addresses the immediate concerns of the borrower but also enhances the overall integrity of the mortgage lending process, ensuring compliance with regulatory requirements and fostering trust in the mortgage industry.

Mortgage Company Compliance Obligations

In the realm of mortgage lending, the discovery of material information related to a borrower or supplied by employers plays a pivotal role in maintaining the integrity and transparency of the mortgage process. Mortgage companies are bound by a strict ethical and legal framework that mandates the accurate reporting of any material information that could influence the lending decision. This obligation is not only a cornerstone of ethical lending practices but also a regulatory requirement designed to protect consumers and ensure the fairness of the mortgage market.

When a mortgage company uncovers material information about a borrower, whether through the application process, during verification checks, or information supplied by an employer, it must take steps to accurately document and report this information. Material information can include changes in employment status, income levels, debt obligations, or any other factor that could impact the borrower's ability to repay the loan. The accurate reporting of this information is critical, as it directly affects the underwriting process and the determination of the borrower's creditworthiness.

The process of reporting discovered material information begins with a thorough documentation of the information itself. Mortgage companies must establish clear protocols for recording the details of the information discovered, including the source, date of discovery, and any actions taken in response. This documentation serves multiple purposes: it provides a record for internal review and compliance checks, supports the underwriting decision, and, if necessary, forms part of the disclosure to the borrower.

Transparency with borrowers is another critical aspect of reporting material information. Mortgage companies are required to inform borrowers of any significant information that may affect their loan application or terms. This disclosure must be made in a timely manner, allowing borrowers the opportunity to respond or provide additional information. The principle of transparency ensures that borrowers are fully informed about the status of their application and any factors that may influence the lending decision.

Moreover, mortgage companies must also navigate the regulatory landscape that governs the disclosure of material information. Various federal and state laws, including the Truth in Lending Act (TILA), the Real Estate Settlement Procedures Act (RESPA), and regulations enforced by the Consumer Financial Protection Bureau (CFPB), set forth specific requirements for the disclosure of material information to borrowers. Compliance with these regulations is not optional; mortgage companies must ensure that their policies and procedures for reporting material information align with legal standards to avoid regulatory penalties and safeguard consumer rights.

In addition to regulatory compliance, the ethical implications of accurately reporting material information cannot be overstated. Ethical lending practices demand honesty, integrity, and fairness in all aspects of the mortgage process. By adhering to these principles, mortgage companies build trust with borrowers, regulators, and the public. This trust is foundational to the long-term success of any mortgage lending operation, reinforcing the importance of ethical behavior beyond mere compliance with legal requirements.

The obligations of mortgage companies to report discovered material borrower or employer information accurately are multifaceted, encompassing legal, ethical, and operational dimensions. These obligations ensure the integrity of the mortgage process, protect consumer interests, and uphold the principles of fair and transparent lending. Through diligent documentation, transparent communication with borrowers, and strict adherence to regulatory requirements, mortgage companies fulfill their responsibility to report material information, thereby contributing to the overall health and trustworthiness of the mortgage industry.

Relationships with Consumers

Protecting Consumer Data and Cybersecurity

In the realm of mortgage lending, the ethical handling of personal information and cybersecurity measures are paramount to maintaining trust and integrity in relationships with consumers. Mortgage Loan Originators (MLOs) and lending institutions are entrusted with sensitive personal and financial information, making it imperative to implement robust cybersecurity protocols to protect this data from unauthorized access, breaches, and cyber-attacks. The foundation of these protocols includes the deployment of advanced encryption methods for data transmission and storage, regular cybersecurity training for all employees, and the adoption of multi-factor authentication (MFA) to secure access to systems containing consumer information.

Disclosing conflicts of interest is another critical aspect of ethical conduct in the mortgage industry. MLOs must proactively identify and disclose any potential conflicts of interest that could influence their recommendations or decisions regarding loan products. This includes personal or financial interests in properties, relationships with real estate agents, builders, or sellers, and any incentives or commissions tied to specific loan products. Transparency in disclosing these conflicts ensures that consumers can make informed decisions based on unbiased information, reinforcing the trust between MLOs and their clients.

The process of requesting credit reports is governed by the Fair Credit Reporting Act (FCRA), which stipulates that MLOs must obtain explicit borrower consent before accessing their credit reports. This consent should be documented in writing, clearly explaining the purpose of the credit inquiry and how the information will be used. It is essential for MLOs to communicate the potential impact of credit inquiries on consumers' credit scores, especially the distinction between hard and soft inquiries. Hard inquiries, typically triggered by a formal loan application, can affect the borrower's credit score, whereas soft inquiries, used for pre-qualification purposes, do not. By ensuring informed consent, MLOs uphold ethical standards and respect the borrower's rights and privacy.

In implementing these practices, MLOs and lending institutions not only comply with legal requirements but also demonstrate a commitment to ethical behavior and consumer protection. The secure handling of personal information, transparent disclosure of conflicts of interest, and respectful acquisition of credit reports are fundamental to building and maintaining trust in the mortgage lending process. These practices are integral to fostering positive relationships with consumers, characterized by mutual respect, integrity, and professionalism.

Disclosing Changes and Validating Eligibility

In the dynamic landscape of mortgage lending, Mortgage Loan Originators (MLOs) are frequently confronted with scenarios that necessitate adjustments to down payments or offered interest rates. These changes are often precipitated by fluctuations in the market, revisions in the borrower's financial status, or the discovery of new information during the loan processing phase. Ethical practice and regulatory compliance mandate that MLOs disclose any such changes to borrowers in a clear, timely, and transparent manner. This ensures that borrowers are fully informed and can make decisions based on the most current and accurate information available.

The validation of powers of attorney (POA) represents another critical aspect of mortgage transactions, particularly in situations where a borrower cannot be present to execute necessary documents. The POA grants an individual—the attorney-in-fact—the authority to act on behalf of the borrower in legal or financial matters pertaining to the mortgage. MLOs must rigorously verify the authenticity and scope of the POA document to ensure it is legally valid and accurately reflects the borrower's intentions. This involves confirming that the POA is durable, meaning it remains in effect even if the borrower becomes incapacitated, and checking that it specifically authorizes the attorney-in-fact to engage in the mortgage transaction. The validation process may require consultation with legal counsel to ensure compliance with state laws and lender policies, safeguarding against potential fraud and protecting the interests of all parties involved.

The inclusion of non-resident co-borrowers in mortgage applications introduces additional layers of complexity, necessitating thorough verification of their eligibility and compliance with lending regulations. Non-resident co-borrowers, who may be citizens of another country or residing in the U.S. without permanent residency status, can impact the loan's risk assessment and underwriting criteria. MLOs must navigate a maze of regulatory requirements, including verifying the co-borrower's income, credit history, and legal status in the United States. This often involves liaising with immigration authorities, international credit agencies, and legal experts to gather and validate the necessary documentation. Furthermore, MLOs must ensure that the loan product is available to non-resident co-borrowers and that their participation complies with the lender's policies and federal regulations, such as the Patriot Act and the Equal Credit Opportunity Act (ECOA).

Ensuring compliance in these scenarios requires MLOs to possess a deep understanding of the regulatory landscape, a commitment to ethical practices, and a dedication to serving the best interests of the borrower. It underscores the importance of transparency in the mortgage process, the need for meticulous attention to detail in validating legal documents, and the imperative to navigate the complexities of involving non-resident co-borrowers. By adhering to these principles, MLOs uphold the integrity of the mortgage industry, foster trust with consumers, and contribute to the smooth execution of mortgage transactions.

Income Verification and Ethical Practices

In the realm of mortgage lending, the verification of income accuracy stands as a cornerstone of ethical practice and due diligence. Mortgage Loan Originators (MLOs) are tasked with the critical responsibility of ensuring that all income reported by a borrower is accurate, verifiable, and reflective of their true financial situation. This process involves a meticulous review of financial documents, including tax returns, W-2 forms, pay stubs, and bank statements. In cases of unreported or fluctuating income, MLOs must employ a heightened level of scrutiny, often requiring additional documentation or explanations to reconcile discrepancies. The aim is to construct a comprehensive and truthful picture of the borrower's income, safeguarding against the approval of loans that exceed the borrower's repayment capabilities.

Documenting gifts and unexplained deposits presents another layer of complexity in the mortgage application process. Gifts, often received from family members towards the purchase of a home, require clear documentation through gift letters. These letters must specify the amount of the gift, the relationship between the donor and the recipient, and a statement affirming that the gift is not a loan and does not need to be repaid. Similarly, unexplained deposits into a borrower's account necessitate a thorough investigation to source and verify the origins of these funds, ensuring they are not undisclosed loans or other financial obligations that could impact the borrower's ability to repay the mortgage.

Maintaining ethical relations with appraisers is paramount in the mortgage industry. MLOs must navigate these interactions with integrity, ensuring that no undue influence or pressure is exerted to inflate property valuations. The independence of the appraisal process is protected by strict regulations and guidelines, which mandate a separation between the loan production staff and the appraiser to prevent conflicts of interest. Ethical MLOs facilitate transparent and unbiased appraisals, respecting the appraiser's professional judgment and adhering to all applicable laws and standards.

Handling multiple loan applications requires a fair and impartial approach, ensuring that each borrower is assessed based on the merits of their application without bias or preferential treatment. This involves a systematic review process where each application is evaluated against the lender's criteria, regulatory requirements, and the principles of fair lending. MLOs must manage these applications with diligence, ensuring timely and equitable processing to maintain the trust of applicants and uphold the integrity of the lending institution.

Throughout these processes, MLOs play a crucial role in upholding ethical standards and regulatory compliance. By verifying income accuracy, documenting gifts and deposits correctly, maintaining impartial appraiser relations, and treating all loan applications with fairness, MLOs contribute to the integrity of the mortgage lending process. This commitment to ethical practices not only protects consumers but also reinforces the trust and confidence in the financial system, fostering a stable and equitable mortgage market.

Truthful Marketing and Advertising Compliance

Ensuring truthful, non-deceptive marketing and adhering to permissible claims in advertising are foundational to maintaining ethical standards and compliance with federal advertising regulations within the mortgage industry. Mortgage Loan Originators (MLOs) and their associated institutions are bound by a legal and ethical obligation to present information in a manner that is both accurate and not misleading to consumers. This commitment is governed by several federal laws and regulations, including but not limited to the Truth in Lending Act (TILA), the Real Estate Settlement Procedures Act (RESPA), and regulations enforced by the Consumer Financial Protection Bureau (CFPB).

Permissible Statements in Advertising: Advertising materials must accurately reflect the terms, conditions, and costs associated with mortgage products. This includes presenting an Annual Percentage Rate (APR) that is calculated in accordance with TILA regulations. The APR must encompass not only the interest rate but also any points, fees, and other charges that the borrower is required to pay to obtain the mortgage, providing a comprehensive view of the loan's cost.

Furthermore, any claims regarding the benefits of a particular mortgage product must be substantiated, ensuring that they do not mislead the consumer about the product's true nature. For instance, if an advertisement promotes a "no-cost" mortgage, it must clearly delineate what is meant by "no-cost." Typically, this means that while there may be no upfront costs paid directly by the borrower at closing, these costs may be incorporated into the loan's interest rate or amortized over the loan's term.

Compliance with Federal Advertising Regulations: The CFPB's Regulation Z, which implements TILA, stipulates specific requirements for mortgage advertising. These requirements include clear and conspicuous disclosure of loan terms and conditions, and prohibitions against misleading representations about government endorsement, the nature of the interest charged, and the potential for default.

Advertisements must not contain misleading statements or omit important information that could mislead the consumer about the nature or terms of a credit product. For example, if an advertisement features a low introductory interest rate, it must also clearly disclose that this rate is subject to increase and under what conditions. Similarly, if there are restrictions on the availability of advertised terms, these restrictions must be clearly noted.

Non-Deceptive Marketing Practices: Non-deceptive marketing practices extend beyond the mere accuracy of information to include the overall impression that advertising materials may convey. This means considering not only the explicit claims made in an advertisement but also the inferences that a reasonable consumer might draw from them. For instance, if an advertisement emphasizes the ease and speed of obtaining a mortgage without equally highlighting the importance of credit qualifications, it could mislead consumers about their likelihood of approval.

Ensuring Compliance: To ensure compliance with these complex regulatory requirements, MLOs and their institutions should implement rigorous review processes for all advertising and promotional materials. This may involve legal review and ongoing training for staff involved in marketing and advertising efforts. Additionally, institutions should establish clear internal guidelines that align with federal regulations, promoting a culture of compliance and ethical advertising practices.

By adhering to these principles and regulatory requirements, MLOs and mortgage institutions not only protect consumers but also uphold the integrity of the mortgage lending process. This approach fosters trust in the financial system and contributes to a stable and fair mortgage market, aligning with the interests and objectives of ambitious and ethical professionals within the industry.

General Business Ethics

In the realm of mortgage loan origination, the integrity of information provided by both borrowers and mortgage loan originators (MLOs) is foundational to ethical business practices. Falsified information, whether from the borrower or the MLO, undermines the trust essential for the functioning of the financial system and can lead to significant legal and financial repercussions. Addressing such falsifications requires a robust framework that includes preventive measures, detection mechanisms, and corrective actions.

Preventive measures involve thorough training for MLOs on the importance of accuracy in all documentation and communication. This training should cover the legal implications of falsifying information, the ethical standards expected within the industry, and the potential consequences for both the individual and the organization. For borrowers, clear communication about the necessity of providing accurate and truthful information, along with the potential consequences of falsification, can deter attempts to provide false information.

Detection mechanisms are critical in identifying falsified information as early as possible. These can include cross-verifying information provided by borrowers with independent sources, conducting random audits of MLO-submitted applications, and implementing software that can flag inconsistencies or anomalies in application data. When falsified information is detected, a structured process should be in place for investigating the issue, determining the extent of the falsification, and taking appropriate corrective action.

Corrective actions can range from additional training and warnings for minor first offenses to termination and legal action for more serious or repeated falsifications. It is crucial that the response be proportionate to the severity of the falsification and that it sends a clear message about the organization's stance on ethical behavior.

Giving solicited or unsolicited advice is another area where ethical considerations are paramount. MLOs must ensure that any advice given is in the best interest of the borrower and not influenced by the potential for personal gain. This means providing clear, accurate, and complete information about loan products, terms, and conditions, and helping borrowers understand how different options could impact their financial situation. MLOs should also be trained to recognize when it is appropriate to refer borrowers to other professionals, such as financial advisors or attorneys, for advice beyond the scope of mortgage lending.

Protecting borrower confidentiality against outside inquiries is a fundamental ethical obligation for MLOs. This includes securing personal and financial information provided by borrowers during the loan application process and ensuring that such information is only shared with parties who have a legitimate need to know, in accordance with privacy laws and regulations. MLOs must be vigilant in safeguarding this information, employing strong cybersecurity measures to prevent unauthorized access and being cautious in their communications to avoid inadvertent disclosures.

Addressing falsified information, providing ethical advice, and protecting borrower confidentiality are critical components of general business ethics in mortgage loan origination. These practices not only comply with legal standards but also build trust with borrowers, which is essential for the long-term success of any financial institution. By adhering to these ethical standards, MLOs and their organizations can contribute to a more transparent, fair, and trustworthy mortgage lending industry.

Conclusion

Acknowledgments

We extend our deepest gratitude to you, our readers, for selecting this guide as your companion on the path to mastering the NMLS SAFE MLO Exam. Your dedication to professional growth and excellence in the mortgage industry is both commendable and inspiring. It is a reflection of your commitment to not only advancing your own career but also to contributing positively to the broader financial landscape. This journey, while challenging, is enriched by your determination, focus, and ethical standards.

Your choice to engage with this material speaks volumes about your ambition and your drive to achieve personal and professional milestones. The complexities of the mortgage industry require a steadfast approach to learning and adaptation, qualities that you have demonstrated by embarking on this educational endeavor. The landscape of real estate and finance is ever-evolving, and your willingness to stay informed and compliant with the latest regulations and best practices is crucial to your success and the well-being of the consumers you will serve.

We recognize the diverse backgrounds from which you come and the varied levels of expertise you bring to this field. It is our hope that this guide has served as a bridge, connecting you to the knowledge and skills necessary to excel in your role as a mortgage loan originator. Your resilience and persistence in navigating through the intricate content of this guide are a testament to your commitment to excellence.

As you move forward in your career, remember that the principles and knowledge acquired here are foundational elements that will support your continued growth and success. The real estate and finance sectors are dynamic and challenging, but with the preparation and understanding you have gained, you are well-equipped to navigate them with confidence and integrity.

Thank you for allowing us to be a part of your professional journey. Your success is a reflection of your hard work, and we are honored to have contributed to your preparation for the NMLS SAFE MLO Exam.

Encouragement and Motivation in Mortgages

The mortgage industry, with its ever-evolving landscape, demands a high level of **ethical commitment**, **continuous learning**, and **adaptability** from mortgage loan originators (MLOs).

Success in this field is not just about passing exams or meeting licensing requirements; it's about building lasting trust with clients and upholding the integrity of the financial system. **Ethical practices** are the cornerstone of a reputable MLO. This involves more than just adhering to legal standards; it means prioritizing the client's best interests, avoiding conflicts of interest, and being transparent in all transactions.

Continuous learning is equally critical. The regulatory environment, loan products, and market conditions change frequently. Staying informed through ongoing education and professional development ensures that you can provide the best advice and service to your clients. This commitment to knowledge not only prepares you for immediate challenges but also positions you as a trusted advisor in the eyes of your clients and colleagues.

Adaptability in the face of change is what separates the good from the great in the mortgage industry. This means being open to new technologies, regulatory changes, and shifts in consumer behavior. Embracing change allows you to identify opportunities for growth and innovation, ensuring that you remain competitive and relevant in a crowded marketplace.

Building **trust** is the ultimate goal. Trust is not given; it's earned through consistent, ethical behavior, a commitment to your client's needs, and a deep understanding of the mortgage process. Your success as an MLO is directly tied to the trust you build with your clients and your ability to navigate them through one of the most significant financial decisions of their lives with competence and care.

By committing to these principles, you not only enhance your professional reputation but also contribute to the overall integrity and success of the mortgage industry. Your role is critical in helping individuals achieve their dreams of homeownership, and by embracing ethical practices, continuous learning, and adaptability, you ensure that those dreams are built on a solid foundation of trust and expertise.

Made in the USA
Las Vegas, NV
03 June 2025